MODELLING THE
MIDLAND REGION
FROM 1948

MODELLING THE
MIDLAND REGION
FROM 1948

COLIN BOOCOCK, TONY CLARKE AND PETER SWIFT

THE CROWOOD PRESS

First published in 2019 by
The Crowood Press Ltd
Ramsbury, Marlborough
Wiltshire SN8 2HR

www.crowood.com

British Library Cataloguing-in-Publication Data
A catalogue record for this book is available from the British Library.

ISBN 978 1 78500 519 0

Acknowledgements
The authors would like to express their grateful thanks to Famous Trains member
Peter R. Stanton, a retired railway electrical engineer, for his input into the sections on
electrification and lighting.

All uncredited photographs and diagrams are by the authors. Photographs by others are
credited in the caption.

The authors have also downloaded a number of items from the internet. Where a
licence does not explicitly cover reproduction, they have made every effort, not always
with success, to trace the copyright holder. Any inadvertent breach of copyright is entirely
unintentional, and copyright holders are asked to contact the publisher with regard to any
fee that may be due.

Frontispiece: On this model of Chinley station, the left bracket signal is set for straight ahead;
this arm is higher than the one that would indicate diversion to the line heading off right. This
bracket signal's base will eventually be buried under the platform surface and the operating
wires made less visible. The other pair of bracket signals that control the exit from the bay
platform are of the same height, indicating routes of equal status.

Typeset by Jean Cussons Typesetting, Diss, Norfolk

Printed and bound in India by Replika Press Pvt Ltd

CONTENTS

PREFACE

When we were first asked to create a book about modelling the London Midland Region of British Railways from 1948, the term 'Midlandness' was coined. It was used to refer to those features of the whole railway that identified the London Midland Region as a distinct entity, and could be reasonably modelled.

My colleagues and I from the Famous Trains Charity Model Railway in Derby will endeavour to outline the historical aspects up to the nationalization and after, with a view to modelling those features still apparent in locomotives, rolling stock, infrastructure and buildings. We will then show how they may be represented accurately in model form.

Whatever stage you are at in creating a model railway – beginning with a train set and building up,

Print of the London & Birmingham Railway's Euston terminus in 1837 showing a train of open carriages, ready to be rope-hauled to Camden, where a locomotive will be attached. Over the next 100 years, Euston grew in a piecemeal fashion, causing confusion to passengers and difficulties for the operating staff.

creating a larger and more realistic model using flexible track and more sophisticated control equipment, or recreating a real place in model form – the more accurate your model, the more convincing it will be. And the more convincing your model, the greater your satisfaction and your enjoyment of the hobby will be.

We will not spend time describing how to design your plan, lay track and ballast, wire up the electrics or choose whether to operate by DCC or analogue control. However, if you wish to create a model based on part of the London Midland Region of British Railways, this book should help you to produce something that is readily identifiable as part of that Region, whether it is freelance or an accurate representation of a real place.

The London Midland Region of British Railways was the largest in area of the Regions created after nationalization. It covered a huge part of England, from London to the north and north-west, to the Scottish borders and the coast of North Wales, through central Wales to the south and into the south-west, overlapping the territory of the Western Region and the Southern. It served huge metropolitan cities and towns, with heavy industry and mass movement of people as well as freight. It ran through scenically outstanding areas such as the Peak District, and into the Lake District. It also followed the North Wales coast to Anglesey and, jointly with the SDJR, ran across Somerset and Dorset, down to the south coast at Bournemouth. The Region as a whole enjoyed a wide variety of scenery, from mountainous areas to the seaside, rolling farmland to giant limestone quarries, and small rural villages to busy industrial towns. Choosing an appropriate setting for a model is vital to creating the feeling of 'Midlandness'.

Unless you have a very large room in which to model, you will almost certainly be limited to modelling one type of area, town or countryside, seaside or small branch line. Wherever you choose, there will be distinct features that will enable you to model your chosen subject in a convincing manner.

With the coming electrification of the West Coast Main Line, old Euston had to go and demolition started. By 26 April 1964, all the later additions had gone, and a new Euston was taking shape behind.

To achieve this aim, we shall begin by providing a detailed and complete account of the locomotives and rolling stock that would have been present on the London Midland Region from its creation in 1948 until 1988. This will include all the items that are available to allow you to model accurately in the most popular scales. Realistic models of other prototypes may be created by modifying ready-to-run models or kits. We will show how this may be done using examples that feature on the Famous Trains Model Railway in Derby.

We will then take a look at the necessary parts of the infrastructure directly associated with the railways – stations, and so on – before looking at some scenic ideas that are most relevant to the London Midland Region.

We will also cover signalling, an area often omitted from layouts, partly due to a lack of understanding as to where to place which signals. We will look at headcodes, too, and the positioning of head and tail lamps on trains.

Finally, we have a chapter that is especially for modellers who wish to focus on an area of the London Midland Region where electrification was used as a means of locomotion.

CHAPTER ONE

THE FORMATION OF THE LONDON MIDLAND REGION

The London Midland Region of British Railways was formed in 1948, with the nationalization of the four privately owned companies that had run most of Britain's railways since 1923. The LM Region comprised the English and Welsh lines of the London Midland and Scottish Railway (LMS). The LMS also operated in Scotland and Northern Ireland but these lines passed to the Scottish Region and Ulster Transport Authority. The LMS, together with the LNER, Southern and an enlarged GWR, had been formed in 1923 following a Government-decreed amalgamation of the companies that had owned and run the railways up to that date.

There were a number of adjustments to regional boundaries over the years. By 1950, LMS lines in south Wales had been transferred to the Western Region while the London Tilbury & Southend line had passed to the Eastern Region. The Eastern Region's Great Central main line south of Chesterfield was later transferred to the LM Region, and LM Region lines in West Yorkshire passed to the Eastern Region. By the early 1960s, Western Region lines north of Banbury had passed to the LM Region and LM lines west of Barnt Green (Birmingham) had gone to the Western Region.

Initially, the main change was seen in the responsibility for the day-to day operation of these areas; changes to the pattern of train operation came later.

THE INHERITANCE OF THE LM REGION

The general appearance of most British railway lines in 1960 was that of the pre-grouping company that had owned the line until 1923. The railway infrastructure had matured by 1890 and then remained almost unaltered until the 1960s. The locomotives and carriages got bigger but the lines continued to be signalled by semaphore signals worked from signal boxes at each station, and at intermediate points. After 1923, upper quadrant signals began to replace lower quadrant ones, but the pre-grouping image was still dominant, except for a small number of stations and signal boxes that had been reconstructed by the LMS or by the LM Region.

The LMS was formed by the following pre-grouping companies:

LONDON & NORTH WESTERN RAILWAY

The LNWR had been formed in 1846 by the amalgamation of the London & Birmingham, Manchester and Birmingham and Grand Junction Railways. The GJR had previously absorbed the pioneer Liverpool & Manchester Railway, opened in 1830. The LNWR ran the West Coast Main Line from London (Euston) to Carlisle and served the West Midlands, Lancashire and North Wales. The LNWR operated a number of lines on the Welsh border jointly with the Great Western and had numerous branches,

The LNWR Jacobean-style station building at Bletchley, with overall roof, looking north on 27 July 1963.

Later, stations on the LNWR were cheaply built in timber. This is Dudley Port, looking west on 22 June 1963. Even the platforms are timber and the platform lamps appear still to be gas-lit.

Marshbrook, on the GWR/LNWR Shrewsbury & Hereford Joint line, looking north from a passing test train on 13 May 1987. The station closed in 1957, but the building is still standing on the right, together with the small brick-built LNWR signal box.

Severn Bridge junction signal box at Shrewsbury, photographed on 19 February 2018. Probably the largest mechanical box still in use today, it is an LNWR box, although the adjacent boxes to the south and west are both to GWR designs.

Melton Mowbray station, looking west on 10 August 2017. A feature of many Midland stations was the elegant platform canopy, with hipped ended roofs at right-angles to the track, supported on cast-iron pillars and a brick wall along the rear.

extending its influence widely from Peterborough to South Wales.

MIDLAND RAILWAY

The Midland was formed in 1844 by the amalgamation of three railways centred on Derby. By 1875, the Midland connected London (St Pancras) with the East Midlands, Manchester, Leeds and Carlisle, together with a line from Birmingham to Bristol. The Midland operated joint lines, with other companies, which brought its trains into Liverpool, Bournemouth, Great Yarmouth and South Wales.

Melton Mowbray station on 10 August 2017, showing the brick wall of the canopy attached to Sancton Wood's original Syston & Peterborough Railway station building of 1848.

Appleby station on 22 September 1994, a typical 1875 Settle & Carlisle three-gable single-storey building. The decorative pierced bargeboards appeared elsewhere on the Midland.

Harlington station downside building, on 31 May 2005. This is typical of the stations on the Midland's Bedford–St Pancras line of 1867.

Wellingborough goods shed on 11 August 1990. It is no longer rail-connected and the later extension is gone, enabling the building to be seen. It is on the Midland's 1858 Leicester–Hitchin line.

The Lancashire & Yorkshire Railway's Hebden Bridge station, looking west on 21 July 2008. It had recently been restored, much to its LYR appearance.

LANCASHIRE & YORKSHIRE RAILWAY

The Lancashire & Yorkshire did just what its name implied, operated mainly east–west services in those counties, while the LNWR and Midland generally ran north–south. The LYR had shipping interests on both west and east coasts, at Fleetwood and Goole. The LYR and LNWR amalgamated prior to the grouping, in 1921.

Hebden Bridge signal box on 21 July 2008. It is a typical LYR box with a timber superstructure on a brick base. The window in the gable end was also used on the Great Central and Wirrall boxes.

Blackpool Central station on 8 September 1962. The main station is on the right, with excursion platforms on the left. It all went shortly after when the line was cut back to Blackpool South.

LMS-built 3F 0-6-0T No. 47635 shunting the goods depot at Bradford Exchange on 18 August 1960. The LYR's Bradford goods depot is a typical large city goods depot, with paving between the tracks. Visible wagons are all either vans or open merchandise wagons; coal must have been handled elsewhere. It would have looked this way for the previous sixty years.

NORTH STAFFORDSHIRE RAILWAY

The North Staffordshire Railway, based in Stoke on Trent, had a North–South line from Macclesfield to Stafford, which was used by some LNWR Manchester–London trains, together with an east–west line from Derby to Crewe, and numerous branches.

A Class 120 DMU on the 14.30 Derby–Crewe passing the North Staffordshire Railway crossing cottage at Eggington on 18 August 1974.

Tutbury Crossing signal box on 11 August 2017. This was built by signalling contractor McKenzie & Holland in the 1870s for the North Staffordshire Railway, although with the windows much altered. Other NSR boxes on the Derby–Stoke line had timber superstructures with gable ends.

FURNESS AND MARYPORT & CARLISLE RAILWAYS

The Furness railway connected the LNWR and the Midland at Carnforth to Barrow in Furness and then ran north around the Cumbrian coast to

A Class 47 leaving Arnside on the 16.05 Crewe–Barrow on 2 September 1980. The Furness Railway included three estuary crossings in its meander from Carnforth to Whitehaven, including the River Kent at Arnside. Six Mark 1s form a typical train on the secondary Furness Railway route.

The Furness Railway station at Haverthwaite on 28 September 1984.

Whitehaven. The oldest constituent company of the LMS was the tiny Maryport & Carlisle Railway, formed in 1838 to serve the West Cumberland coalfield. An outlying LNWR line from Whitehaven to Maryport completed the coastal route from Carnforth to Carlisle.

WIRRALL, MERSEY AND OTHER ABSORBED RAILWAYS

The Wirrall Railway operated suburban services from New Brighton and West Kirby to Seacombe, with a ferry connection to Liverpool, and to the Mersey Railway at Birkenhead. The Mersey Railway

The Wirrall Railway's Birkenhead North station on 16 April 2003. Until 1937, this would have been the interchange point between Mersey Railway electric trains and LMS (Wirrall) steam trains.

Birkenhead North signal box on 3 August 1993.

DECLINE AND BELATED RENAISSANCE

All these railways operated numerous branch lines, some of which were built by the railway companies, while others were promoted by towns that had not been rail-served. The aim was to reap the benefits of reduced transport costs for the town, rather than for the branch line itself to be a money earner. These lines were generally worked by, and later taken over by, the larger company to which they connected. The structures on such lines were frequently not built to the standard railway company designs.

With the development of mechanized road transport in the early twentieth century, cheaper alternative transport became available. Closure of branch lines had already started before the end of the First World War and more occurred in the 1930s. Closures of branch lines and intermediate stations on through lines began to accelerate during the 1950s and became rampant in the 1960s, following the recommendations of the British Railways Board report 'The Reshaping of British Railways', in 1963. Up to that date, British Railways had been under a statuary requirement to operate within its income but, during the 1970s, the need for state support of 'socially necessary' railway services was accepted. Population movement and road conges-

ran from Liverpool, under the Mersey, and connected with the Wirrall and with the GWR/LNWR joint line to Chester. After briefly operating with steam traction, the Mersey Railway was electrified in 1903 and retained its independence until 1948. In 1938, the Wirrall lines were electrified and train services integrated with those of the Mersey Railway.

In addition, there were a number of small companies, which did not add materially to the overall picture of the LMS or LMR.

LMS signal box at Melton Mowbray on 10 August 2017. LMS timber boxes were an amalgam of LNWR and Midland styles. This one displays a feature that should be useful to modellers who are short of width. The lever floor is carried forward over the track to the end loading dock.

tion have recently led to the reopening of some stations and lines, but most of these have occurred since the disappearance of the Regions.

The old railway companies, both pre- and post-1923, were responsible not only for running the trains but also for the acquisition and maintenance of their infrastructure, locomotives and rolling stock, together with ancillary services such as road cartage, steamship services and hotels. The Regions of British Railways continued to manage all these functions. The old railway companies had also owned canals and had invested in many of the larger regional bus companies, but these were transferred to other subsidiaries of the British Transport Commission in 1948.

In 1986, the British Railways Board set up new business sectors to run its passenger and freight services, which would be responsible for their own infrastructure, traction and rolling stock. The three passenger sectors were InterCity, to run the long-distance trunk services, Network South East, to run suburban services out of London, and Regional Railways, to run the rest of the passenger services.

Freight sectors included Freightliner, Trainload Freight and Parcels. The business sectors took responsibility for train services in 1986 but it took about two years to set up the organizations needed for them to control their own infrastructure and

Manchester Oxford Road station on 1 April 1989. When a new station was required for terminating trains from Altrincham in 1960, the location of the station on an embankment precluded anything heavy, so this laminated timber roof was put up.

Uttoxeter signal box on 11 August 2017. Uttoxeter had been a major junction on the North Staffordshire railway but, by the 1960s, had been reduced to just a double track line with two refuge loops. The existing signal boxes were replaced by a new box to the current LM Region design.

rolling stock. It was therefore late 1988 before the LM Region finally disappeared. The ancillary services – cartage, shipping, hotels, and so on – all passed out of railway ownership and control.

THE CORPORATE IMAGE 1: BRITISH RAILWAYS

There may have been relatively few new stations and other railway buildings erected during the British Railways period, but those that were already there required maintenance, painting and provision of signage. This enabled the imposition of the corporate image of the railway administration. The initial British Railways colour schemes for railway buildings involved a combination of light (usually cream or white) and dark, with the latter chosen to differentiate between the Regions. These were dark blue on the Eastern, Crimson Lake on the LM, orange on the North Eastern, light blue on the Scottish, green on the Southern and brown on the Western Region. The colours were applied to all timber and ironwork on buildings, lamp posts, signs, and so on. Enamelled 'sausage' totems carrying station names were fixed to station lamps and existing name boards were either repainted or replaced by new ones.

THE CORPORATE IMAGE 2: BRITISH RAIL

In 1964, the British Railways Board adopted the trading name 'British Rail' and a totally new corporate image. Regional colours were out, to be replaced by shades of grey, and name boards became white with black lower-case lettering. The British Rail Double Arrow logo appeared at every possible location and was so successful that it was copied by a number of European railways. It has long outlasted British Rail and is still used on signposts outside railway land to show the way to the nearest station.

THE CORPORATE IMAGE 3: SECTORIZATION

The business sectors quickly introduced their own corporate images for trains, although with little immediate change to the buildings and infrastructure. An exception to this was the almost overnight appearance of red lamp posts at Network South East stations.

Inevitably, greater image changes occurred with privatization in the 1990s, but those are beyond the scope of this book.

CHAPTER TWO

LONDON MIDLAND AND SCOTTISH LOCOMOTIVES

In 1948, British Railways received 7,850 steam loco-motives, of 112 classes, from the LMS. Twenty-six of the locomotive classes were LMS designs and the rest were pre-grouping. The LMS also provided British Railways with seventy diesel shunters, one main-line diesel locomotive, three diesel railbuses, one 3-car diesel train, two steam railcars, two battery electric shunters and 257 electric motor cars. The majority of the LMS locomotives went to the LM Region, but about 1,300 went to the Scottish Region, together with the three diesel railbuses and one of the two steam railcars. During the British Railways period, further steam locomotives to LMS designs were built between 1948 and 1951, followed by British Railways standard types between 1951 and 1960. The last steam locomotives were taken out of service in 1968.

Only those locomotive types that ran on the LM Region in any significant numbers will be described here. Ready-to-run models of most are available; current model availability is checked against *Model Rail*'s publication *Britain's Model Trains 2017*.

THE LMS CHIEF MECHANICAL ENGINEERS

It is usual in railway enthusiast circles to ascribe each class of locomotive to the man who was Chief

Royal Scots Fusilier No. 46103 leaves Chinley on its way to London with the 'Palatine', on the Famous Trains layout.

Mechanical Engineer (CME) at the time it was designed. Design of locomotives was only one of the many responsibilities of a CME; some delegated design work almost entirely to their drawing office staff, while others kept a closer personal hand on locomotive design. However, it was the CME's signature that finally authorized production.

During its twenty-five years of existence, the LMS got through six CMEs, compared with three on the LNER and two each on the GWR and Southern. Three of the LMS CMEs gained knighthoods, only one for his railway work.

George Hughes had been the CME of the L&Y and his seniority over the others gained him the LMS appointment (1923–1925). His main contribution to LMS motive power was the Class 5 'Crab' 2-6-0.

Sir Henry Fowler had been the Midland CME and had gained his knighthood for his wartime work for the Government. He was basically a production engineer with an interest in metallurgy and left design matters to the drawing office. During his period as CME (1925–1931), Midland designs proliferated but a few more modern designs also appeared, including an excellent 2-6-4T and the Royal Scot 4-6-0s.

Ernest Lemon was another production engineer. During his brief tenure (1931–1932), his main activity was to carry out an analysis of the maintenance costs of each type of locomotive, and to reorganize the LMS locomotive servicing and maintenance departments. He later became a Vice President of the LMS and was awarded his knighthood for reorganizing aircraft production for the RAF in 1938.

William Stanier came from the GWR and brought together the best features of GWR and LMS practice. His most important contributions to LMS motive power (1932–1944) were the Class 5 4-6-0, 8F 2-8-0s and the Duchess 4-6-2s. He was knighted in 1942.

Charles Fairburn (1944–1945) came from English Electric and had been the Chief Electrical Engineer of the LMS. His main interest was in developing diesel electric traction and he left steam matters in the hands of his successor. George Ivatt was

Fairburn's assistant for steam development. His main contributions to the LMS (1945–1947) were the post-war Class 2 and Class 4 2-6-0s, 2-6-2Ts, and the 'Fairburn' 2-6-4T.

SHED CODES AND POWER CLASSIFICATIONS

All British Railways steam locomotives carried an oval plate at the base of the smokebox, which showed the shed allocation of the locomotive. This was a Midland Railway feature, extended by the LMS and adopted by British Railways. A Derby-based locomotive, for example, would be marked '17A'. For London Midland Region locomotives, shed codes 1 to 12 were Western Division (ex LNWR) sheds, 14 to 22 were Midland Division and 23 to 26 were Central Division (ex L&Y) sheds. The missing 13 was not due to superstition about an unlucky number; the 13 sheds became Eastern Region 33s with the transfer of the LT&S line in about 1950. Sheds 30 to 49 were Eastern Region, 50 to 54 North Eastern, 60 to 68 Scottish, 70 to 75 Southern and 80 to 89 Western Regions. The Western Region 84 and 89 sheds passed to the LM Region in 1963.

Power classifications 1 to 4 were introduced by the Midland in the early 1900s and adopted by the LMS, with 1 identifying the smallest locomotives and 4 the biggest. This would allow for the later introduction of larger types. The LMS introduced F and P suffixes for freight or passenger work and British Railways later introduced the suffix MT for mixed traffic locomotives. In 1948, classifications 1 to 8 were in use, including the odd 5XP for the Patriot and Jubilee 4-6-0s. In 1952, the 5XPs, 6Ps and 7Ps became 6Ps, 7Ps and 8Ps. Class 0 was introduced for a number of previously unclassified small locomotives.

LOCOMOTIVE LIVERIES

In 1948, most LMS locomotives were painted unlined black, although there were still a few red ones around and, from 1946, the 7P 4-6-2s and 5XP and 6P 4-6-0s were painted with maroon edging and cream lining to their black livery. Initial British Railways repaints continued the LMS liveries but with 'BRITISH RAILWAYS' lettering in place of 'LMS'. A few early repaints have M prefixes to their LMS numbers. After a few experimental liveries, British Railways adopted the following liveries in late 1948:

- Dark blue with white/black/white lining: Class 7P 4-6-2s (1949–1951 only).
- GWR-style dark green (Middle Chrome Green but frequently referred to as Brunswick Green) with orange/black/orange lining: Class 5XP and 6P 4-6-0s, also 7P 4-6-2s from 1951.
- LNWR-style black with red/cream/grey lining: smaller passenger engines and mixed traffic engines. Some 7P 4-6-2s, and 5XP and 6P 4-6-0s also carried this livery briefly, when repainted at Crewe in 1948–1949.
- Unlined black: all goods engines and some mixed traffic engines in the mid-1960s.

Initially, these liveries were applied with BRITISH RAILWAYS lettering but the first British Railways emblem, with a lion standing over a wheel, was applied from late 1949. The lion faced forward on both sides of the locomotive. In 1957, the second BR emblem was introduced, with the lion upright, holding a wheel. This was the crest of the coat of arms of the British Transport Commission, and should always face left, although forward-facing crests were applied on both sides until late 1958.

In 1957, LMS red was reintroduced for the LM Region Class 4-6-2s, by then classified 8P. Initially, this had BR-style lining but was later seen with LMS-style black edging with a single cream line.

In the following sections, dealing with individual classes of locomotive, it can be assumed that the BR livery was unlined black, unless another livery is shown.

PRE-GROUPING LOCOMOTIVES

Generally, the pre-grouping locomotives inherited by the LM Region continued to run on the lines of their original railway, although there were a few exceptions.

LONDON & NORTH WESTERN RAILWAY

Although the largest constituent of the LMS, only two classes of LNWR locomotive ran on the LM Region in any numbers. LNWR locomotives showed up badly in Lemon's maintenance cost examination

Ex-LNWR Super D 0-8-0 No. 49361 leaving Birmingham New Street on a rail tour of local lines on 22 June 1963. 49361 was built as LNWR class B 4-cylinder compound 0-8-0 1289 in 1903. It was rebuilt as a Class G1 2-cylinder 0-8-0 in 1921 and as a G2A in 1938.

and suffered the full weight of the LMS 'Scrap and Build' policy in the 1930s. No LNWR express locomotives survived long enough to receive the LNWR lined black livery, when it was reintroduced in late 1948.

The LNWR Super D 0-8-0s

The main LNWR contribution to the LM Region was made by 470 0-8-0s of LNWR classes G1, G2 and G2A, generally known as Super Ds, numbered between 48892 and 49454. These were the survivors of 572 locomotives built between 1892 and 1922 of classes A to G. The G1s were rated 6F; some were built new from 1912 but most were rebuilt from older locomotives. The 7F rated G2s were built from 1922 and the G2As were rebuilds of G1s to G2 standard. They worked mainly on ex-LNWR lines and the last few came out of service in 1964. An unusual feature was that they were never fitted with smokebox door number plates.

G2 49395 was retained by the National Railway Museum (NRM) collection and has been returned to service on heritage railways.

An OO gauge model is produced by Bachmann.

The LNWR 'Coal Tank' 0-6-2Ts

300 'Coal Tank' 0-6-2Ts were built by the LNWR between 1881 and 1896. Sixty-four remained in service in 1948 and worked local passenger and goods trains on ex-LNWR lines, numbered between 58880 and 58935. Some were fitted to work push-pull trains. Many of the last survivors were based in South Wales, by then on the Western Region.

The last survivor 58926 was withdrawn from Abergavenny in 1958 and was displayed for some years at Penrhyn Castle, Bangor. It has since been returned to service on heritage railways.

An OO gauge model has recently appeared from Bachmann.

MIDLAND RAILWAY

The Midland was the second-largest constituent of the LMS and, including Midland designs built by the LMS, contributed by far the largest number of pre-grouping locomotives to the LM Region. The

Midland's last Chief Mechanical Engineer, Sir Henry Fowler, became the CME of the LMS from 1925 to 1931 and continued the production of four Midland locomotive types as LMS standard classes. Midland Railway engines were driven from the right side of the cab, but the LMS engines built from 1928 were driven from the left. The Midland-built locomotives generally remained on their own territory but the LMS built ones roamed over most of the LMS system, with many passing to the Scottish Region in 1948.

Class 2P 4-4-0s

Between 1912 and 1923, Derby Works built 143 Class 2 4-4-0s. Although classified as rebuilds of earlier locos, they were totally new, apart from the tenders. Between 1928 and 1932, a further 138 were built, by the LMS, with left-hand drive. Most came to British Railways as 40400–40562 (Midland) and 40563–40700 (LMS).

In LM Region days, the 2Ps were used mainly on local passenger and parcels trains or as station pilots. They were also added as pilots to main-line

Midland Compound 4-4-0 No. 1000, restored to its 1914 condition in 1958, arriving at Skipton on an RCTS excursion from Leeds to Ravenglass on 4 September 1960, for what might have been a last chance to ride on the line. No. 1000 worked the special from Leeds to Carnforth and from Penrith for the return to Leeds via the Settle & Carlisle line. Unknown to each other, two of the authors of this book were on that train and agree that 1000 gave an exemplary performance.

IMPROVING A HORNBY RAILROAD COMPOUND

When the Bachmann models of Midland compound 4-4-0s were launched in 2013 – No. 1000 painted in 1960s Midland Railway livery and 41157 in BR lined black – one of the trustees of the Famous Trains charity was critical of certain details. In particular, it was clear from a photograph he had taken in 1960 that the chimney of the real No. 1000 was the original MR shape, with curved sides rather than the parallel sides as modelled in LMS form by Bachmann (although that would have been right for the BR-liveried one). He was also of the opinion that, for such a high price, the model should have had a fall-plate covering the wide gap between the engine and the tender.

For less than half the price it was possible to buy a new Hornby Railroad model of the LMS red compound 1000. This model formerly had tender drive, but in 2013 had locomotive drive and traction tyres on the leading coupled wheels, so its haulage ability was beyond doubt. Famous Trains forked out £54 for this model and gave it a thorough inspection once it was out of the box.

Hornby Railroad prices are kept competitive sometimes by using much older body moulds that are reasonably accurate, and also by simplifying the painting and attached details. Hornby does not skimp on the mechanisms in Railroad models, which we understand are the same as in their more expensive, detailed models. One particular attraction of the Railroad compound was the closeness of its chimney shape to the original Midland Railway design, as carried by No. 1000 in its 1960 preserved and operational state.

To make the model suitable in detail to run on the Chinley model railway at Famous Trains, several improvements were needed:

- We glued a plastic sheet fall-plate to cover the gap between the engine and tender, and stuck a model crew inside the rather open cab.
- The front wheel splashers on the prototype (fitted by the Midland Railway to avoid splash-back from a pilot locomotive on water troughs) would be needed on the model. To avoid collision with the bogie front, we cut small plastic sheet rectangles and stuck them, not to the buffer beam, but to the bogie frame front.
- The 'LMS' on the tender was removed and replaced by the number '1000'. We used T-Cut to remove the 'LMS' transfers, and took figures from an HMRS sheet for the '1000' on the tender sides.
- The '1000' on the cab side was replaced by the Midland Railway crest, which was also on the HMRS transfer sheet, as were the letters 'M' and 'R' that we placed on the front buffer beam.

The Hornby Railroad model straight out of its box.

The model No. 1000 after improvement work.

- The coupling rods were rearranged to fit on the crank pins 'outside' the connecting rods. We got the crank pins out with a nut runner, and fitted washers to bring the coupling rods further out.
- The bulky front coupling was not needed and was sawn off.
- While the overall Crimson Lake livery was approximately correct, the black lining adjacent to the cream lining was missing, and several areas that should have been painted black were actually crimson. Cream lining was missing around the buffer beam. These omissions were hand-painted in acrylic. The whole locomotive body was later varnished with gloss and matt acrylic where required.
- A Springside model headlamp was fitted, LMS type, which we painted black with crimson sides.

None of this was difficult to achieve for someone with a steady hand.

Compared with a scale compound 4-4-0, our Railroad model is slightly longer, due to a longer coupled wheelbase that most people do not notice. The tender is also slightly too big as its model forebears in previous decades contained the motor (now hidden in the engine). Otherwise, Hornby have done a grand job with the model shape and details, and our upgrade has been, we feel, very successful.

In service, the only problem we have faced has been that one of the traction tyres came off, due we suspect to someone dragging the locomotive along the track unpowered and stretching the tyre. We used a replacement tyre from Hornby's pack of spare tyres for the Southern T9 4-4-0, which has similar-sized wheels.

No. 1000 in service with Famous Trains at Chinley.

expresses that were over the allowed weight for the train engine. They were painted in the BR lined black livery.

The last Midland engines were withdrawn in 1963 and the last LMS ones in 1964.

Airfix produced an OO gauge model of the LMS Class 2P, with tender drive, in 1984 and it is now produced, with loco drive, by Hornby.

Class 4P Compound 4-4-0s

In 1901, Johnson built five large 3-cylinder compound 4-4-0s for the Midland Railway. Deeley built forty more, to a modified design, between 1905 and 1909 and the five Johnson engines were rebuilt to the Deeley design. Between 1924 and 1932, the LMS built another 195 compounds, with minor variations from the Midland design, including left-hand drive on the later ones. All passed to British Railways and they were numbered 41000–41044 (Midland engines), 41045–41100 and 40900–40939 (LMS engines).

During British Railways days, they were used mainly on semi-fast or local passenger trains, and carried the lined black livery. The last Midland engine was withdrawn in 1953 and the last LMS one in 1961. 41000 was retained for the national collection and restored to its 1914 state as Midland No. 1000. It was returned to service in 1960 for working special trains, but has not run now for some years.

Hornby produced an OO gauge model of 1000, in LMS livery, with tender drive in 1981, and it is now produced, with loco drive, in Hornby's Railroad range. Bachmann also produce a model, available in both Midland and LMS versions, although not reflecting all the differences between the two types. Graham Farish used to produce an N gauge model, with a rather oversized boiler.

Class 2F and 3F 0-6-0

Between 1873 and 1903, the Midland built 865 inside-framed 0-6-0s of Class 2, followed between 1903 and 1908 by seventy Class 3 engines, with larger boilers. Many of the Class 2 engines later were reboilered as Class 3. From 1916, new boilers with Belpaire fireboxes were introduced in both small and large form.

Ex-Midland 3F 0-6-0 No. 43637 on a local trip goods train in Chaddesden sidings, Derby, on 11 May 1963. It is carrying Class K head signals for a stopping goods train.

In 1948, British Railways acquired 391 3F 0-6-0s numbered between 43174 and 43833, and ninety-five 2F 0-6-0s, which were renumbered 58188–58310. By 1948, the 3Fs were all similar in appearance, apart from some of the earlier ones having smaller wheels. The 2Fs were less consistent, with a few retaining round-top fireboxes and two types of cab being fitted. In British Railways days, the 2F 0-6-0s were used on local goods trip working, particularly on lines with restricted axle loading. The 3Fs were used widely on goods working, together with some local passenger train work. The last 3Fs were withdrawn in 1964.

An OO gauge model of a Class 3F 0-6-0 in LMS or BR state is produced by Bachmann.

Class 4F 0-6-0

Between 1912 and 1921, Henry Fowler built 192 Class 4 0-6-0s, which were a development of the Class 3 with a superheated boiler and piston valves. Between 1924 and 1941, a further 580 were obtained by the LMS. Engines built from 1928 had left-hand drive. All passed to British Railways in 1948. The Midland ones became 43835–44026 and the LMS ones 44027–44606.

In British Railways days, 4Fs were used widely on goods trains, with some passenger work. The last Midland-built engines were withdrawn in 1965 and the last LMS built one in 1967. Four are preserved on heritage railways.

LMS-built 4F 0-6-0 No. 44235 at Burton on Trent on a southbound Class K coal train on 11 May 1963. LNER B1 4-6-0 61004 is about to uncouple from an RCTS special from St Pancras to Buxton and back.

Airfix produced a model of an LMS 4F in 1978, with tender drive, and it is now produced by Hornby, with loco drive and other improvements. Bachmann also produce a 4F model of the ex-Midland Railway version in OO gauge whilst Graham Farish produce an N gauge model. Lima produced an O gauge model of a 4F in the 1970s.

Class 1F 0-6-0T

280 Class 1F 0-6-0Ts were built for the Midland Railway between 1874 and 1900. Ninety-five passed to British Railways in 1948 and were numbered between 41660 and 41895. Some retained round-top boilers and some Belpaire; some had full cabs, while others only had the front part of the cab. They were used for shunting work, with five being retained at Barrow Hill until 1966 for shunting at Stavely Ironworks. 41708 was bought for preservation and has run on a number of heritage railways.

An OO gauge model of a 1F 0-6-0T is produced by Bachmann in both open- and closed-cab versions.

Class 3F 0-6-0T

Sixty larger 0-6-0Ts with power classification 3 were built by the Midland Railway between 1899 and 1922. Most were built with round-top boilers but, from 1919, they all received Belpaire boilers.

The LMS built another 422 3F 0-6-0Ts between 1924 and 1931, including seven for the S&DJR, which differed in that they had screw reverse. The LMS 3Fs differed from the Midland engines in having extended smokeboxes and bunkers. Sixty Midland and 412 LMS engines came to British Railways in 1948. The Midland engines were numbered 47200–47259 and the LMS ones between 47260 and 47681.

In British Railways days, 3Fs were used almost exclusively on shunting work or short-distance goods trip working. The last Midland engines were withdrawn in 1966 and the last LMS ones in 1967. Ten were bought by heritage railways.

An OO gauge model of an LMS 3F 0-6-0T was first produced by Tri-Ang in the 1950s and Hornby have produced numerous subsequent models with progressive improvements. OO gauge 3F 0-6-0Ts are currently available from both Hornby and Bachmann, whilst Graham Farish have an N gauge model. An O gauge model is due from Dapol.

Class 1P 0-4-4T

Between 1875 and 1900, the Midland Railway built 205 0-4-4Ts for local passenger work and a further thirteen were built for the S&DJR. Sixty-five 1P 0-4-4Ts passed to British Railways in 1948 and sixty-two were renumbered 58030–58091. Some had round-top boilers and others Belpaire. The LMS built a batch of ten 2P 0-4-4Ts in 1932, which were a development of the Midland design.

In British Railways days, the 1P 0-4-4Ts were used on local passenger work, including push-pull trains, for which some were fitted with vacuum-operated control of the engine's regulator from the cab of the push-pull driving coach. They carried the lined black livery and the last was withdrawn in 1960.

An OO gauge model of the 1P 0-4-4T is due to be produced by Bachmann, in a variety of forms.

LANCASHIRE & YORKSHIRE RAILWAY

The Lancashire & Yorkshire Railway was the third-largest English constituent of the LMS. A few of the larger LYR locomotives came to British Railways, but had all gone by 1951. A number of smaller LYR locomotives had rather better staying power.

LYR 2P and 3P 2-4-2Ts

Between 1889 and 1911, the L&Y built 329 2-4-2Ts to work its many short-distance passenger services. Some were built or rebuilt with superheated Belpaire boilers. The earlier engines were classi-

50636 was allocated to a Midland shed (Manningham) in the 1950s but was not push-pull fitted, although the model has had the LMS vacuum control gear fitted, using bits of brass and wire.

fied 2P by the LMS and the superheated ones 3P. A total of 110 2P and 14 3P 2-4-2Ts came to British Railways, numbered between 50621 and 50953 and carrying the lined black livery.

In British Railways days, most were still operating in Lancashire and Yorkshire but some had moved to LNWR or Midland sheds while others had gone

LYR 2-4-2T No. 50636 on a push-pull train at Darley Green, the branch-line terminus of Famous Trains' Chinley layout. 50636 is the Hornby model and the push-pull set is modified from Graham Farish models.

to North Wales. They were used on local passenger services, with some being fitted with push-pull control gear. The last 3P was withdrawn in 1952 and the last 2P in 1961. The first one to be built is preserved in the NRM collection.

Bachmann produce an OO gauge model of an LYR 2P 2-4-2T.

LYR 0F 0-4-0ST

Between 1886 and 1910, the LYR built sixty small 0-4-0STs for shunting at confined locations. Twenty-three came to British Railways in 1948 and were numbered between 51202 and 51253. A number of others were still around, having been sold to industrial users.

In British Railways days, they were used at locations where larger engines would not fit, such as Liverpool and Goole docks. Their small size made them useful off the LYR system and examples turned up at Bath, Burton and Derby, among other places. The last was withdrawn in 1963 and two are preserved, 51218 and LMS 11243, which had been sold to industry before 1948.

The LYR 'Pug' was one of the OO gauge static models produced by Rosebud Kitmaster in the 1950s, and produced subsequently by Airfix and Dapol. Dapol also produced a ready-to-run OO gauge model in the 1980s, which is now produced by Hornby. Little licence is required to run one on any layout with tight curves (how many have not got these?), either as a BR loco or as an industrial.

LMS STEAM LOCOMOTIVES

This section deals with new designs of steam locomotive produced for the LMS. The LMS got off to a bad start, with continued production of undersized Midland designs and with the General Superintendent, Motive Power Superintendent and Chief Mechanical Engineer failing to reach agreement on what was required. Once these problems had been overcome, there was much continuity of design of locomotives through successive CMEs. These will be dealt with according to their use –

express passenger, mixed traffic, goods, passenger tank engines, and so on – rather than by CME.

Largely due to departmental infighting, there was no immediate action to produce a new standard LMS express passenger locomotive design. On the West Coast Main Line something bigger than a 4P compound and with lower maintenance and fuel costs than the LNWR Claughton Class 4-cylinder 4-6-0s was required. Finally, in 1926, the North British Locomotive Company was asked to design and build 'something comparable to a Great Western Castle, but with only three cylinders'. The result was the Royal Scot class.

ROYAL SCOT CLASS 6P 4-6-0S

Seventy Royal Scots were built, 6100–6149 by NBL in 1927 and 6150–6169 at Derby in 1930. Fortunately for the LMS, they did everything that was required of them, apart from a tendency for fuel and water consumption to rise due to piston valve ring wear. In 1935, a further Royal Scot No. 6170 was built, using the chassis of an experimental compound 4-6-0 with a two-stage high-pressure boiler, but now fitted with a large Class 2A taper boiler, and numbered 6170. The rest of the Royal Scots were rebuilt with 2A taper boilers between 1943 and 1955.

In 1948, British Railways received forty-three Royal Scots with taper boilers and twenty-eight with the original boilers, all having taper boilers by 1955. Five went to the Scottish Region. They were numbered 46100–46170 and reclassified 7P in 1952. They carried the British Railways lined green livery, although this was carried by few of the parallel boiler ones before they were reboilered.

The Royal Scots were always main-line engines, built for the West Coast Main Line. After reboilering, they were also allocated to the Midland main lines. As diesel locos were introduced in the 1960s, they began to appear more frequently on parcels or fast goods trains. They were withdrawn between 1962 and 1965, but 46100 and 46115 are preserved.

Both Airfix and Mainline produced OO gauge models of Royal Scots in the 1980s. A parallel boiler Royal Scot is currently available from Bachmann, as

Royal Scot Class 4-6-0 No. 46117 Welsh Guardsman passing Saltaire on the down Thames Clyde express, on 21 August 1960. The train is composed of BR Mark I stock in maroon livery but with an Eastern Region Thompson corridor third in crimson and cream at the front.

is a taper boiler one from Hornby, together with an N gauge taper boiler one from Graham Farish.

PATRIOT CLASS 5XP 4-6-0S

The Patriot Class 4-6-0 was introduced in 1930 as a 3-cylinder replacement of the LNWR Claughton Class 4-6-0s, using the large parallel boiler that had been fitted to some Claughtons in the 1920s. The result was a smaller version of the Royal Scot, frequently referred to as a Baby Scot, and having power classification 5XP. Two were built at Derby in 1930 and fifty at Crewe and Derby in 1932–34.

Reboilered Patriot Class 4-6-0 No. 45523 (Bangor), with nameplates removed, passing Leighton Buzzard on an Up extra express of LMS carriages on 27 July 1963.

Eighteen were rebuilt with the large 2A taper boiler between 1946 and 1949 and were classified 6P.

British Railways took over forty-five parallel boiler Patriots and eight with taper boilers in 1948, with ten more being fitted with taper boilers by 1949. They were numbered 45500–45551 and all were allocated to the LM Region. Power classification was altered to 6P (parallel boiler) and 7P (taper boiler) in 1952 and the livery was lined green. All were initially allocated to Western Section sheds but some moved to the Midland later. They were always main-line engines, with the parallel boiler 6Ps generally working lesser trains than the 7Ps. The parallel boiler engines were withdrawn in 1960–62 and the taper boiler ones in 1961–65.

None are preserved but a replica parallel boiler Patriot is now under construction.

OO gauge models of Patriots have been produced in both parallel boiler and taper boiler forms by Mainline and Bachmann, using the same chassis as the Royal Scot models. Currently, Bachmann and Hornby both produce parallel boiler Patriots and Hornby also produce the taper boiler version.

JUBILEE CLASS 5XP 4-6-0S

In 1934, another batch of 5XP 4-6-0s was introduced, with Swindon-style taper boilers, smaller than the ones fitted later to the Royal Scots. There

Jubilee Class 4-6-0 No. 45562 Alberta at Skipton on the 06.40 Birmingham–Glasgow on 12 August 1967. This was a summer-only train and Holbeck shed retained 45562 and 45593 Kolhapur to work it between Leeds and Carlisle during their final year of service.

were initial steaming problems until Stanier reconciled Swindon practice with LMS requirements. A total of 191 Jubilees were built at Crewe, Derby and NBL in 1934–36. Two were fitted with the larger Royal Scot boiler in 1942 and were identical to the taper boiler Patriots.

In 1948, British Railways inherited 189 small boiler and two large boiler Jubilees, which were numbered 45552–45742, the large boiler ones being 45735/6. Sixteen Jubilees were allocated to the Scottish Region in 1948. The power classification was altered to 6P (small boiler) and 7P (large boiler) in 1952 and livery was lined green.

LM Region Jubilees were allocated to Western (LNWR), Midland and Central (LYR) division sheds, so appeared widely over LMR main lines, including the Midland's West Road to Bristol. Mainly on express passenger work, they appeared on more menial tasks latterly. In 1952, 45637 was destroyed in the Harrow accident, and the others were withdrawn between 1960 and 1967. Four are preserved, 45593, 45596, 45690 and 45699.

Using the same chassis as the Royal Scot and Patriot, OO gauge models of Jubilees have been produced by Mainline and Bachmann. A small boiler Jubilee is available from Bachmann. Rivarossi produced an N gauge Jubilee for Peco many years ago and one is currently available from Graham Farish.

PRINCESS ROYAL CLASS 7P 4-6-2S

When William Stanier became the LMS CME in 1932, there was a need for more powerful locomotives for the Scottish expresses. The first two Princess Royals 6200-6201 were built in 1932. They were clearly based on the GWR King 4-6-0s, with set back outside cylinders, but with four sets of valve gear and a wide firebox, carried on a trailing truck. Following successful trials, ten more (6203–6212) were built in 1935. The number 6202 was given to an experimental turbine-driven locomotive, based on a Princess Royal chassis.

In 1948, British Railways inherited twelve standard Princess Royals and the Turbomotive, which were numbered 46200 to 46212 and all allocated to the LM Region. In 1952, their power classification was altered to 8P. In 1950, the Turbomotive 46202 needed a replacement turbine and was rebuilt with conventional cylinders. It returned to service in 1952 but was damaged beyond repair in the Harrow accident a few months later.

Always West Coast Main Line engines, in the British Railways period the Princess Royals were used mainly on Scottish or Liverpool expresses. They were withdrawn from service in 1961/2 and 46201 and 46203 are preserved.

A rather crude OO gauge model of a Princess Royal Pacific was produced by Tri-Ang in the 1950s, and subsequently made available in various improved forms. Hornby have more recently produced very much better models of the class, but they are not in the 2017 catalogue.

CORONATION (OR DUCHESS) CLASS 7P 4-6-2S

The Coronation or Duchess was a development of the Princess Royal, with a larger boiler, larger wheels and with the outside cylinders moved forward. The first five were built in 1937, with streamlined casings and a blue livery, to work the Coronation Scot high-speed service. Between 1938 and 1948, 6225–6229 and 6235–6248 were built with streamlined casings and 6230–6234 and 6249–6256 and 45257 without. Most of the streamlined ones had lost their casings by 1948 and all had received double chimneys.

British Railways received three streamlined and thirty-four conventional locos, with one conventional loco under construction. They were numbered 46220–46257 and nine were allocated to the Scottish Region. The last streamlined loco lost its casing in 1949 and the power classification was changed to 8P in 1952. Livery was blue or green, with sixteen of the LM allocation later receiving the red livery. They were always West Coast Main Line locos, generally on the Scottish expresses, and were withdrawn in 1962–64.

46229, 46233 and 46235 are preserved. 6229 has had its streamlined casing replaced, for display at the National Railway Museum.

4mm scale models of the Princess Coronations have been available for almost as long as the locomotives themselves. Hornby Dublo produced a very good model, for its time, of 6231 Duchess of Atholl in 1939, but it only became available after the war. Hornby produced a slightly short tender-drive model of a streamlined loco in the 1980s and have more recently come up with better models of both streamlined and conventional locos for OO gauge (although the streamlined version is not currently in the catalogue). A new model of the conventional version is under development. An N gauge model is available from Graham Farish.

There are only three mixed-traffic tender engines to consider: the Hughes and Stanier Class 5 2-6-0s and the Stanier Class 5 4-6-0. The Ivatt Class 4 and Class 2 2-6-0s were considered by the LMS to be goods engines, although both classes did a lot of passenger work in British Railways days.

THE HORWICH CLASS 5 2-6-0

George Hughes, the LYR Chief Mechanical Engineer, became the first CME of the LMS. A 2-6-0 mixed-traffic locomotive, suitable for use on the whole LMS system, was designed at Horwich, incorporating many features from recent LYR designs. It was coupled to standard Midland tenders, which were narrower than the cab and platform of the engines. With their high-set cylinders, designed to clear the loading gauge, they were known as 'Crabs'.

All came to British Railways in 1948. They were numbered 42700–42944 and carried the lined black livery. Sixty-four went to the Scottish Region. They were used primarily on main-line goods work but with considerable passenger work as well, particularly on summer extra trains.

A tender-drive model of a Horwich 2-6-0 was produced by Lima in the 1970s, but its cab was narrowed, to match the tender, which was itself too long. A much better OO gauge model was later produced by Bachmann and is still available.

Duchess Class 4-6-2 No. 46251 City of Nottingham near Shrivenham on a return RCTS excursion from Nottingham to Eastleigh and Swindon, on 9 May 1964.

Class 5 'Crab' 2-6-0 No. 42862 leaving Bradford Exchange station on 8 August 1960 on empty coaching stock. The width mismatch between loco and tender is very apparent.

THE STANIER CLASS 5 2-6-0S

When William Stanier came to the LMS, there were requests for more Horwich 2-6-0s but Stanier decided to take the opportunity to introduce his own ideas. The Stanier 2-6-0s had many features of the Horwich 2-6-0s but, by using a higher boiler pressure, Stanier was able to introduce smaller cylinders and reduce their width, allowing the cylinders to be placed in line with the wheel centres. The 2-6-0s were the first LMS locomotives to be fitted with taper boilers. Forty were built at Crewe in 1933–34.

The forty Stanier 2-6-0s passed to British Railways in 1948 and were numbered 42945–42984. In British Railways days, all were allocated to the Western Division of the LM Region and received the lined black livery. Although classified as mixed-traffic locomotives and working occasional excursions, they were mainly used on goods trains. They were withdrawn from service between 1963 and 1967. 42968 is preserved on the Severn Valley Railway.

An OO gauge model of a Stanier Class 5 2-6-0 is available from Bachmann.

THE STANIER CLASS 5 4-6-0S

Following Ernest Lemon's analysis of locomotive maintenance costs, it was apparent that what the LMS really wanted was a single type of locomotive that would go anywhere and do anything. The Stanier Class 5 4-6-0 was as near to this dream as anyone was likely to get, and the LMS had confidence enough to order 472 straight off the drawing board, with no prototype testing. Between 1935 and 1938, forty-five came from Crewe, 100 from the Vulcan Foundry and 327 from Armstrong Whitworth. Construction started again in 1943 and a total of 842 were built. They were numbered, in order of building, 45000–45499, 44800–44999 and 44758–44799. In 1950, around 600 were allocated to sheds in all parts of the LM Region, while about 230 were on the Scottish Region and some were at ex-LMS sheds on the Southern (S&D) or Western Regions. Livery was lined black.

Inevitably, they were not all the same. Early steaming problems led to a change to the firebox design and there were variations in the positioning of domes and top feeds. These variations moved from one locomotive to another as boilers were exchanged. 44767 was fitted with outside mounted Stephenson valve gear, 44738–44757 had Caprotti valve gear and 44686/7 had a later form of Caprotti valve gear. A number of the late Class 5s had roller bearings, requiring a small increase in the coupled wheelbase. 44765/6 had double chimneys.

They worked just about every type of train, goods and passenger, and were likely to turn up any-

Class 5 4-6-0 No. 44990 near Stanningley on a Leeds–Manchester train on 3 September 1960. The train consists of four LMS corridor carriages, led by a Period 1 brake composite from the late 1920s.

where, except the smaller branch lines. They were withdrawn from service between 1961 and 1968. Eighteen are preserved, all of which were built for the LMS, including 44767, which was fitted with the Stephenson valve gear.

A fairly crude OO gauge model of a Class 5 4-6-0 was produced by Graham Farish in the 1950s and there has generally been a Class 5 model in Hornby's list from the 1970s on. Hornby currently produce an OO gauge Class 5 4-6-0 in their standard range and continue to produce an earlier model, at a lower price, in the Railroad range. An N gauge model is available from Graham Farish.

The LMS produced three series of passenger tank engines: Class 4 2-6-4Ts, in four varieties, for heavier work, and Class 3 and Class 2 2-6-2Ts for lighter duties.

FOWLER CLASS 4 2-6-4TS

Between 1927 and 1934, 125 2-6-4Ts with parallel boilers (2300–2424) were built at Derby for suburban passenger work. At a time when most of Derby's products were more than a little outdated, these benefited from the current thinking on valve-gear design and proved to be extremely sprightly performers. Most had a Midland-style cab

but 2395–2424 had more modern cabs, with side windows and doors.

All came to British Railways in 1948 and were renumbered 42300–42424. They were used on short-distance passenger work in most parts of the LM Region, with some going to ex-LMS Scottish or Western Region sheds. They were withdrawn between 1959 and 1966. Livery was lined black.

An OO gauge model of a Fowler 2-6-4T has been produced by Hornby since the 1980s. A much improved version was introduced in 2002 and is currently still available.

STANIER 2-CYLINDER CLASS 4 2-6-4TS

Following a batch of 3-cylinder 2-6-4Ts for the Tilbury line, which all passed to the Eastern Region, Stanier returned to 2-cylinder 2-6-4Ts with taper boilers for general use on the LMS. Between 1936 and 1943, 206 (numbered 2425–2494 and 2537–2672) were built at Derby and by the North British Loco Co in Glasgow (2545–2617).

All came to British Railways as 42425–94, 42537–42672 and all were allocated to various parts of the London Midland Region for short-distance passenger traffic. Livery was lined black. They were withdrawn between 1960 and 1967.

Fowler Class 4 2-6-4T No. 42360 passing Kensington Olympia on the West London line on a short transfer parcels train, on 11 February 1961.

Stanier 2-cylinder Class 4 2-6-4T on empty stock duties at Euston in June 1960.

Hornby have produced an excellent OO gauge model of the Stanier 2-6-4T but it is not in the current catalogue.

'FAIRBURN' CLASS 4 2-6-4T

Between 1945 and 1951, 277 'Fairburn' 2-6-4Ts were built, with a shorter coupled wheelbase than the earlier 2-6-4Ts. They were numbered 42050–42299 and 42673–42699, the latter being built first. Most were built at Derby but 42066–42106 were built at Brighton for use on the Southern Region; they were later exchanged for BR Standard 2-6-4Ts. About 100 of the Fairburn 2-6-4Ts went to

'Fairburn' Class 4 2-6-4T 42072 approaching Bradford Forster Square on the Bradford carriages of the Devonian on 15 August 1960.

Scotland but most of the rest were at LM Region sheds, for short-distance passenger work. Livery was lined black.

They were withdrawn between 1961 and 1967. Two, both from the Brighton batch, 42073 and 42085, but withdrawn from Yorkshire sheds, are preserved.

Bachmann produce an OO gauge model of a Fairburn 2-6-4T and Graham Farish an N gauge model.

CLASS 3 2-6-2T

For lighter local passenger work, Derby built 209 Class 3 2-6-2Ts between 1930 and 1938, which became BR 40001–40209. 40001–70 had parallel boilers and 40071–209 taper boilers. Most were based at various LM Region sheds for local passenger work but about twenty of the taper-boilered ones went to Scotland. Livery was lined black. They were withdrawn between 1959 and 1962.

There is no ready-to-run model available.

IVATT CLASS 2 2-6-2T

The Ivatt Class 2 2-6-2T was a purpose-built modern tank engine for branch-line operation. Ten locomotives, 1200–1209, were built at Crewe in 1946–47 and were followed by another 120, British

Ivatt Class 2 2-6-2T No. 41226 at Amlwch on the 10.35 to Bangor, formed of a single push-pull coach, on 9 July 1964. This was a summer-only steam working in 1964.

Railways 41210–41329, in 1948–52. 41210–41229, 41270–41289 and 41320–41329 were fitted with the LMS vacuum-control push-pull gear. 41240–43 and 41290–41319 went new to the Southern Region, and were followed in the early 1960s by 41320–41329. Most of the rest were based at various LM Region sheds for local passenger, goods and station pilot work. Livery was lined black.

They were withdrawn between 1962 and 1967. Four of the Southern Region locos, 41241, 41298, 41312 and 41313, are preserved on heritage railways.

Bachmann produced an OO gauge model of a Class 2 2-6-2T in 1995, which was ahead of its time in quality and has kept up well with further improvements. A push-pull version has been produced, but will probably need a bit of finding. Dapol produce an N gauge model.

STANIER CLASS 8F 2-8-0

The first of William Stanier's 8F 2-8-0s was built at Crewe in 1935 and, by 1939, 126 were in service on the LMS. On the outbreak of the Second World War, the 8F 2-8-0 was adopted as the standard goods locomotive for the Ministry of Supply and by the wartime Railway Executive Committee. Further 8Fs were built by the LMS workshops,

Class 8F 2-8-0 No. 48649, with 3,500-gallon tender, leaving Bletchley on a southbound Class F express goods train on 27 July 1963. 48649 was one of thirty-nine 8Fs that exchanged tenders with Jubilees in the late 1950s.

private locomotive builders and by the workshops of the GWR, LNER and Southern Railways. By 1946, 852 had been built, many of which were sent abroad.

British Railways ultimately received 666 8F 2-8-0s, including 128 that had been working on the LNER as Class O6, but were transferred to the LMS in 1947. The final two were transferred from the War Department in 1957. They were numbered between 48000 and 48775 and allocated mainly to LM Region sheds for goods work. Livery was unlined black.

They were withdrawn from service between 1960 and 1968. Eight are preserved on heritage railways, including one that has returned from Turkey.

A model of an 8F was produced by Hornby Dublo in the 1950s and a tender-drive one came from Hornby in the 1980s. A new loco-drive OO gauge model appeared in 2003 and is currently available. Graham Farish produce an N gauge model.

IVATT CLASS 2 2-6-0

The Ivatt Class 2 2-6-0 was designed as a replacement for the 2F 0-6-0 and was, effectively, a tender version of the Class 2 2-6-2T. The first twenty appeared in 1946–47 as LMS Nos 6400–6419, and the remaining 108 as British Railways 46420–46527 in 1948–1953. 46400–46464 were built at Crewe, 46465–46494 at Darlington and 46503–46527 at Swindon. With a few exceptions, 46400–46459 and

46483–46502 were allocated to the LM Region, 46460–46464 to Scotland, 46465–46482 to the Eastern Region and 46503–46527 to the Western, although many of these returned to the LM Region in the 1960s. They were widely used on goods and passenger work on the longer branch lines or as station pilots. Livery was lined black, although some of the Western Region ones were painted green in the late 1950s.

They were withdrawn between 1961 and 1967 and seven are preserved, being ideal for heritage railways.

Bachmann produce an OO gauge model and Graham Farish one in N gauge.

IVATT CLASS 4 2-6-0

The Ivatt Class 4F 2-6-0 was designed as a replacement for the 4F 0-6-0. The first locos appeared as LMS 3002–3010 and a total of 162 were built between 1947 and 1952 as British Railways 43000–43161. 43000–43049 and 43112–43136 were built at Horwich and 43050–43111 and 43137–43161 at Doncaster. 43000–43049 were built with double chimneys but these were replaced by single chimneys in the mid-1950s. Generally, the Horwich-built ones were allocated to the LM Region and the Doncaster ones to the Eastern Region. 43132–43141 went to the Scottish Region. Although conceived as goods engines, they were later classified as mixed traffic

Class 2 2-6-0 No. 46480 at Buxton shed on 11 May 1963.

Class 4 2-6-0 No. 43021 passing Leighton Buzzard on the down slow line on a Class K goods train on 27 July 1963.

and carried the lined black livery, although they were used mainly on goods work.

They were withdrawn between 1963 and 1968; 43106 is preserved.

Bachmann produced an OO gauge model in 2005, which is currently still available.

The main goods tank engine built by the LMS was a derivative of a Midland design. The only others were three small classes, only one of which is described here.

SENTINEL SHUNTERS

Sentinel shunting locomotives, with the vertical boilers used in Sentinel steam wagons, were bought by a number of railways and industries from the 1920s to the 1950s. The LMS bought five, to two different designs, in 1930–31, for use at specific locations. They were numbered 7180–7184. Two more, 7191 and 7192, came to the LMS from the Somerset & Dorset. They became British Railways 47180–47184, 47190 and 47191, and were used at locations requiring small locomotives, so can be justified on many model railways. They were withdrawn in 1953–56.

An OO gauge model of a Sentinel shunter, as used by the LNER and LM Region 47180–47183, has been produced by Dapol and is available from *Model Rail* magazine.

THE LMS GARRATT 2-6-0+0-6-2TS

In 1927–30, the LMS bought 33 2-6-6-2T Garratt articulated locomotives from Beyer Peacock, primarily for coal traffic from the East Midlands to London. They came to British Railways as 47967–47999 and were based at Toton and Hasland, working coal trains to London and over the Hope Valley line. They were withdrawn in 1955–58.

In 2014, Heljan produced an OO gauge model of an LMS Garratt for sale by Hattons. It is not currently available.

LMS DIESEL LOCOMOTIVES

The LMS tried out a variety of small diesel shunting locomotives in the 1930s, but the only ones to reach British Railways service were three versions of a large diesel electric shunter. Two survive in preservation, after use by the army and industry. Two batches of larger 0-6-0 diesel shunters (7069–7079) were bought from Hawthorn Leslie & Co in 1934–35, with 300hp engines and two traction motors. These were followed in 1939–42 by forty 0-6-0 shunters numbered 7080–7119, with English Electric 350hp engines, with a single motor driving the wheels through a jackshaft and connecting rods. They were withdrawn between 1961 and 1967.

No ready-to-run model is available.

DERBY/ENGLISH ELECTRIC 2-MOTOR DIESEL SHUNTERS

In 1944, the LMS returned to the more compact 2-motor drive arrangement and built 116 diesel shunters with English Electric 350hp engines and power equipment between 1944 and 1952. 12033–12102 were allocated to the LM Region and 12103–12138 to the Eastern Region. Virtually identical locomotives were built by the LNER (BR 15000–3), GWR (15101–15106) and SR (15201–15203), and English Electric (Dick Kerr Works) built 100 for the Netherlands Railways (NS) between 1949 and 1957.

With a maximum speed of 20mph, they were limited to shunting work at the larger railway centres. Livery was initially unlined black but, from 1956, repaints were in green and a few received the corporate blue livery. They were given TOPS Class 11 but were never renumbered, although some received a D prefix to their 12xxx numbers.

They were withdrawn between 1967 and 1972 and a number were sold for continued use by industry. One of the original WD batch and a number of the BR locos are preserved and have been joined by some of the NS locos.

No OO scale model of the class has been produced, but an HO scale model of one of the NS ones was made in Austria by Roco. Resin bodies are also available for mounting on the chassis of ready-to-run OO gauge models of the similar British Railways 08 Class locos.

LMS MAIN LINE CO-COS 10000 AND 10001

In 1946, the LMS and English Electric agreed to build a pair of 1,600hp Co-Co main-line diesel electric locomotives. Progress was rapid and the first loco, 10000, entered service on 13 December 1947, complete with LMS lettering. It was the first main-line diesel locomotive to run on a British railway and, for such a new venture, was remarkably trouble-free. Its sister 10001 followed on 5 July 1948, without the LMS lettering. Livery was black with silver painted bogies and roof and stainless-steel lettering and waistband.

Initial operation of 10000 was between St Pancras and Manchester but, from October 1948, 10000+10001 also worked as a pair on the Euston-Glasgow line. The Southern Region had also built three main-line diesel locos and, in March 1953, the

LMS Diesel Electric Co-Co 10000 at Chinley on its trial run, with dynamometer car attached, from St Pancras to Manchester in December 1947. 10000 is the Hattons model and the dynamometer car a Stevenson Carriages kit. The train of LMS Period 3 carriages is made up of Airfix, Bachmann, Dapol, Hornby and Replica Railways models.

two LMR locos were transferred to the Southern, working out of Waterloo with the Southern ones. All five moved to the LM Region in 1955 and were used mainly on outer suburban trains from Euston. 10000 was withdrawn in 1963 and 10001 in 1966, having spent its last years on works trains for the Euston electrification. Latterly, they were painted green with orange-black-orange waist lining.

Neither 10000 nor 10001 was preserved, but moves are afoot to produce a replica, as many of the components are common to those used later on other locomotives.

A model of 10000/10001 was produced by Dapol for Hattons a few years ago, followed by a better one from Bachmann. Neither is in the current catalogue.

MAIN LINE BO-BO 10800

In 1946, the LMS agreed to the production of an 800hp Bo-Bo diesel locomotive for branch-line and secondary passenger and goods work. British Thompson Houston (BTH) would provide the elec-trical equipment, Davey Paxman the 827hp diesel engine and the North British Locomotive Co (NBL) the locomotive structure.

The single locomotive entered service in July 1950, numbered 10800. It operated at various locations on the LM Region until it was transferred to the Southern Region in August 1952, followed by a period on the LT&S section of the Eastern Region. It returned to the LM Region in February 1955 and was based at Rugby for local passenger and goods work. Livery was unlined black, initially with silver painted bogies.

It was withdrawn from service in 1959 and sold to Brush Traction Ltd at Loughborough for development work on AC power generation. Tests finished in 1968 and the remains of 10800 were scrapped in 1972.

FELL DIESEL MECHANICAL 2-D-2 NO. 10100

In late 1947, the LMS agreed to the construction of a diesel mechanical main-line locomotive, with

BR's first low-horsepower Bo-Bo diesel electric was number 10800, originally designed and ordered by the LMS. Under the fascinated gaze of two travellers, it is seen in new condition working a test train at Derby in November 1950. W.H.C. KELLAND, COURTESY BOURNEMOUTH RAILWAY CLUB TRUST

a transmission designed by Lt. Col. LFR Fell. No. 10100 was built at Derby and was powered by four Davey Paxman 500hp engines driving a central gearbox through torque converters. Output from the gearbox drove the two centre axles and all four axles were connected by coupling rods. Starting with only one engine working, the others were progressively brought into use as speed increased. The engines were housed in the extended bonnets at either end of the loco, with the gearbox and train heating boilers in the centre.

Trial running started in 1951, after which 10100 worked St Pancras–Manchester expresses. When it worked, it performed well. In 1954, the coupling rods between the two inner axles (already coupled by the gearbox) were removed. 10100 continued in occasional use, mainly on St Pancras–Manchester trains, until late 1958. Livery was unlined black with numbers on the bonnet sides and the BR armorial device in the centre. When additional ventilation grilles were added to the bonnet sides, the numbers were moved inboard of the cab doors.

In 1953, the experimental Fell diesel mechanical 2D2 No. 10100 is seen starting a trial train in the Up direction out of Derby station. The carriages are LMS Stanier main-line stock in BR's carmine red and cream livery. W.H.C. KELLAND, COURTESY BOURNEMOUTH RAILWAY CLUB TRUST

After withdrawal, No. 10100 was sidelined at Derby until the locomotive was dismantled in 1960. This portrait of it in its final condition, with the centre coupled wheels without external coupling rods, was taken on 15 March 1959. W.H.C. KELLAND, COURTESY BOURNEMOUTH RAILWAY CLUB TRUST

CHAPTER THREE

BRITISH RAILWAYS LOCOMOTIVES

Following the nationalization, the boards of Directors of the old railways were replaced by the Railway Executive, which was responsible to the British Transport Commission. Robert Riddles, who had been Stanier's principal assistant on the LMS, was appointed to the Railway Executive with responsibility for mechanical and electrical engineering. Riddles appointed two ex-LMS men as assistants, to be responsible to himself for locomotive design and for construction and maintenance. Ready cash was not freely available, so an early decision was taken to continue to use steam as the main source of traction, as it provided the greatest power for the least capital expenditure. Existing plans for the delivery of more diesel shunting locomotives continued but there were no immediate plans for more main-line diesel locomotives or railcars. Two electrification plans already initiated by the LNER were completed.

WAR DEPARTMENT LOCOMOTIVES

Two classes of steam locomotive that came to the London Midland Region did not come from the LMS, but neither were they British Railways standard designs. They had been built during the Second World War for the wartime Ministry of Supply.

WAR DEPARTMENT 8F 2-8-0 90000–90732

The WD 2-8-0s were designed by Robert Riddles, who was later responsible for the BR Standard locomotives. The idea was to produce a cheaper alternative to the LMS 8F 2-8-0 (see previous chapter) for wartime construction. 935 were built by Vulcan Foundry and the North British Locomotive Co. in 1942–45, 457 of which were loaned to the British railway companies until June 1944, when 932 of them were shipped to Europe. After the war, some remained with European railways but most returned to Britain, where the LNER bought 200 and others were on loan to the British railways. In 1948, the British Transport Commission agreed to buy a further 533, so 733 came to British Railways and were numbered 90000–90732. In 1951, there were about 200 on the LM Region, predominantly

Britannia 70004, 'William Shakespeare' about to depart from Chinley with the southbound 'Palatine' on the Famous Trains model railway.

WD 2-8-0 90516 at Wakefield Kirkgate on an eastbound empty coal train on 4 March 1965. Somewhat surprisingly, it is carrying the Class F express headcode.

in Lancashire and Yorkshire on goods work. Livery was unlined black.

They were withdrawn between 1960 and 1967. All were scrapped, but WD 79257, which became Netherlands Railways No. 1931 and was later sold to the Swedish Railways as No. 4464, was repatriated and has been restored as BR 90733.

Bachmann produced an OO gauge model of a WD 2-8-0 in 1999, which is currently available, and Graham Farish produce an N gauge model.

WD 0-6-0ST, LNER CLASS J94

Between 1943 and 1945, the Ministry of Supply bought 377 0-6-0 saddle tanks, which were to a Hunslet Engine Co. design, but built by a number of manufacturers. Most went abroad but in 1946–47, the LNER bought seventy-five, which were classified J94 and became British Railways 68006–68080. Most remained on the Eastern Region but 68006/12/13/30/34 went to the LM Region for shunting at Birkenhead. They were transferred to the Cromford & High Peak line in the late 1950s and were withdrawn when the line closed in 1966.

None of the British Railways J94s survives, but a number that were sold to industrial users are preserved and some have been painted in British Railways livery.

An OO gauge static model was produced by Rosebud Kitmaster in the 1950s. Dapol produced a ready-to-run OO gauge model in 1984, which is still produced by Hornby, and a better model is produced by DJ Models. An N gauge model was produced by Graham Farish and one is also due from DJ Models. An O gauge model is also due from DJ Models.

BRITISH RAILWAYS STANDARD STEAM LOCOMOTIVES

In the spring of 1948, trials were organized to compare locomotives from the four old companies. However, in the end the new British Railways Standard locomotives owed more to recent LMS practice than to any of the others.

CLASS 7MT BRITANNIA CLASS 4-6-2S 70000–70054

The Britannia Class 4-6-2 was a totally new 2-cylinder 4-6-2 designed at Derby and built at Crewe between 1951 and 1954. All four of the old companies had used multi-cylinder locomotives for their main express types.

Initially, only 70030–34 and 70045–49 were allocated to the LM Region, to Holyhead. In 1958, 70004, 14, 15, 17 and 21 went to Trafford Park for Manchester–St Pancras expresses and, by 1963, all were on the LM Region, mainly at ex-LNWR sheds, working main-line passenger and fast goods trains.

Britannia Class 4-6-2 No. 70031 'Byron' passing Bletchley on an additional express from Blackpool on 27 July 1963. The train is mainly BR Mark I carriages, but with an LMS Period 3 brake second at the front.

They were withdrawn in 1966/67, with 70013 being retained until the end of steam in August 1968. 70000 and 70013 are preserved. Livery was lined green but some ran in unlined green in their final years.

An OO gauge model of a Britannia was produced by Trix in the 1970s and Hornby have had one in their range fairly continuously from the 1980s; the latest version is currently available. Dapol produce an N gauge model.

CLASS 8P 4-6-2 71000 DUKE OF GLOUCESTER

A Class 8P Pacific was considered for inclusion in the initial BR standard range but it was not authorized until LMS Pacific 46202 was damaged beyond repair in the Harrow accident in 1952. 71000 was designed at Derby and built at Crewe in 1954, using many Britannia components but with three cylinders and Caprotti valve gear.

71000 was always based at Crewe, working on the West Coast Main Line. It was never developed to its full potential and was withdrawn in 1962 and retained for preservation. In 1967, one cylinder was removed, for display at the Science Museum in London, and the rest was sold for scrap, but not cut up. In 1974, the hulk of 71000 was bought for preservation and has since been rebuilt and given the development work that it did not receive when new.

Hornby produced an OO gauge model of 71000 a few years ago, which is currently available.

CLASS 6 CLAN CLASS 4-6-2 72000–72009

The Class 6 Clan 4-6-2 was a lighter version of the Class 7, intended for use over the Perth–Inverness line. It was designed at Derby and built at Crewe in 1951–52. 72000–4 were based initially at Polmadie (Glasgow) and 72005–9 at Kingmoor (Carlisle), so all were Scottish Region locos. However, 72005–9 worked regularly over both the Crewe–Carlisle and Settle–Carlisle routes of the LM Region.

The Glasgow locos were withdrawn at the end of 1962 and the Carlisle ones in 1965. Livery was lined green. None was preserved but a replica is being built.

Hornby produced an OO gauge model of a Clan in 2009, which is currently available.

CLASS 5 4-6-0 73000–73171

The Standard Class 5 4-6-0 was designed at Doncaster and built at Derby and Doncaster between 1951 and 1957. Those initially allocated to the LM Region were 73040–49, 73053/4, 73065–74, 73090–99 and 73135–44, but there were numerous later transfers between the Regions. 73125–72154 were fitted with Caprotti valve gear. A variety of tenders were attached.

The LM Region engines were widely spread through the Region and used on a variety of passenger and goods work. Livery was lined black but some Western Region locos later received the lined green livery. They were withdrawn from service between 1964 and 1968 and five are preserved.

An OO gauge model of a Standard Class 5 4-6-0 was produced by Trix in the 1970s. Bachmann produced a much better one in 2002 but it is not in the current catalogue. Graham Farish produce an N gauge model.

BR STANDARD CLASS 4
4-6-0 75000–75079

The Standard Class 4 4-6-0 was designed at Brighton and built at Swindon between 1951 and 1956. Those initially allocated to the LM Region were 75010–19 and 75030–64, being allocated to Lancashire sheds, Bedford and Bletchley, for local passenger and parcels trains. There were numerous later inter-regional transfers and in 1957, the LM had forty-five, scattered around the Region. Some Western and Southern Region Class 4 4-6-0s received double chimneys.

Livery was lined black but most of the Western

Region engines were later painted green. They were withdrawn between 1965 and 1968 and six are preserved.

Mainline produced an OO gauge Standard Class 4 4-6-0 model in 1977 and Bachmann still has its successor in the catalogue. Hornby also produce a Class 4 4-6-0 model.

BR STANDARD CLASS 4
2-6-0 76000–76114

The BR Standard Class 4 2-6-0 was designed at Doncaster and built at Horwich (76000–19, 76075–99) and Doncaster (76020–74, 76100–14) between 1952 and 1957. It was closely based on the LMS Ivatt Class 4 2-6-0. Initially, only 76075–89 were allocated to the LM Region, based in Lancashire and Leicester. Numbers on the LM had increased to thirty-four by 1965, mainly in the Midlands, on local passenger and goods work.

Livery was lined black. They were withdrawn between 1964 and 1967 and four are preserved.

Bachmann produced an OO gauge model of a Class 4 2-6-0 in 2007. It is not in the current catalogue. Graham Farish produce an N gauge model.

BR STANDARD CLASS 2
2-6-0 78000–78064

The BR Standard Class 2 2-6-0 was designed at

Standard Class 4 4-6-0 75056 leaving Linslade tunnel with Bletchley's ex-LNWR breakdown crane on 27 July 1963. It is carrying the Class A headcode.

Derby and built at Darlington between 1953 and 1956. It was closely based on the LMS Ivatt Class 2 2-6-0. 78020–44 and 78055–64 were allocated new to the LM Region, being widely scattered around for local passenger and goods work or as pilots. By 1957, the LM Region had thirty-five locos.

Livery was lined black but the Western Region locos 78000–9 were later painted lined, or unlined green. They were withdrawn in 1964–67 and four are preserved. No ready-to-run model is available.

BR STANDARD CLASS 4
2-6-4T 80000–80154

The BR Standard Class 4 2-6-4T was designed at Brighton and built at Derby (80000–9 and 80054–8), Brighton (80010–53, 80059–105, 80116–154) and Doncaster (80106–15). It was closely based on the LMS 'Fairburn' 2-6-4T, but with modifications to the superstructure to give it a wider route availability. The initial LM Region allocation was 80034–53, 80059–68 and 80081–95, where they were widely scattered, being seen as an addition to the Region's existing fleet of 2-6-4Ts.

In 1959–60, all the LM allocation of BR Standard 2-6-4Ts went to the Southern and Scottish Regions in exchange for 'Fairburn' 2-6-4Ts. In 1963, the LM Region gained fifteen Standard 2-6-4Ts from the Western Region, which were used on ex-Western Region lines. Livery was lined black. They were withdrawn in 1964–67 and fifteen are preserved.

Hornby Dublo produced a model of a Standard 2-6-4T in the late 1950s and Bachmann now produce a much better OO gauge one. An N gauge model is available from Graham Farish.

BR STANDARD CLASS 3
2-6-2T 82000–82044

The BR Standard Class 3 2-6-2T was designed and built at Swindon for use on lines that could not accept the Class 4 2-6-4T. No initial allocation to the LM Region was planned, but 82020 and 21 were sent briefly to Nuneaton for local passenger work. The LM Region later obtained more of the class from the Western Region in 1963, which were moved to Patricroft for local piloting.

Livery was lined black but most of the Western Region ones were later painted green, lined or unlined. They were withdrawn in 1964–67 and none is preserved, although a replica is being built.

Bachmann produce an OO gauge model of the Class 3 2-6-2T, which is currently available. Graham Farish produce an N gauge model.

BR STANDARD CLASS 2
2-6-2T 84000–84029

The Class 2 2-6-2T was designed at Derby and built at Crewe (84000–19) and Darlington (84020–29). It was closely based on the LMS Ivatt Class 2 2-6-2T and all were fitted with the LMS vacuum push-pull control system. 84000–19 were allocated to the LM Region and widely distributed, being virtually identical to the LMS Class 2 2-6-2Ts. In 1961, 84020–29 were also transferred to the LM Region.

Livery was lined black and they were withdrawn in 1964–65. None is preserved and no model is available.

BR STANDARD 9F 2-10-0s 92000–92250

The 9F 2-10-0 was designed at Brighton and built at Crewe (92000–92086, 92097–92177 and 92221–92250) and Swindon (92087–92096 and 92178–92220) between 1954 and 1960. There had been only one British-built 2-10-0 before, a 2-10-0 version of the Riddles WD 2-8-0. Twenty-five of these had come to British Railways, but, as they were all used in Scotland, they will not be described further here.

The 9F 2-10-0 was a larger machine than the WD 2-10-0, designed for faster operation, and was originally conceived as a 2-8-2, a very popular arrangement for fast goods engines in Europe at the time. Time would prove that the decision to build them as 2-10-0s was a good one. It gave them the additional adhesion for moving heavy loads and did not prevent them from running at speeds up to 90mph, although they were officially limited to 60mph.

92020–92029 were fitted with Italian-designed Crosti boilers, incorporating exhaust pre-heating of the combustion air. These had proved to be very suc-

Class 9F 2-10-0 No. 92013 passing Shrewsbury on a southbound Class E goods, with open merchandise wagons at the front of the train, on 4 June 1966.

cessful in improving the performance and economy of Italian locomotives, but showed no saving on the much more modern 9F. 92250 was fitted with the Austrian Giesl oblong ejector, which had improved the economy of Austrian locomotives but provided little advantage on the 9F, compared with the double chimneys fitted to 92000–02/05/06, 92165–167, 92178 and 92183–92249. 92165–92167 were fitted with mechanical stokers for a brief period. 92060–66, 97–99 were fitted with air pumps for use on Tyne Dock–Consett ore trains.

In 1960, the LM Region was allocated 129 9Fs in the number series 92008–33, 92043–59, 92067–96, 92100–139 and 92150–167. Most were working coal trains from the East Midlands to London, over both the Great Central and the Midland main line, but they also worked goods trains over the Midland lines to Bristol, Manchester and Carlisle. Although classified as goods locomotives, they were frequently noted working passenger trains, generally as replacements for the regular motive power.

Livery was unlined black, although the last one to be built, Western Region allocated 92220, was green. The 9F 2-10-0s were withdrawn between 1964 and 1968. Nine are preserved.

Hornby produced a tender-drive OO gauge model of a 9F 2-10-0 in 1971 and a loco-drive version is currently available in Hornby's Railroad range, together with a new model of the Crosti-boilered version. Bachmann also produce an OO gauge model of the standard 9F and an N gauge model is available from Dapol.

BRITISH RAILWAYS DIESEL LOCOMOTIVES

During the early 1950s, British Railways continued the building of diesel shunting locomotives, which had been initiated by the LMS and, to a lesser extent, by the GWR, LNER and SR. A new version of the 350hp diesel electric shunter was introduced, together with a variety of smaller shunting locomotives with mechanical or hydraulic transmission. Initially, these were all numbered in the 1xxxx range. The British Railways 1955 Modernisation Plan brought a wide range of main-line diesel locomotives from a number of British manufacturers, as well as British Railways workshops. Some of these had very short lives, either because of design faults or due to changes in traffic patterns.

In 1957, at the same time as the livery was changed to green, a new BR number series was introduced, with most diesel locomotives being allocated new numbers with a D prefix. Pre-nationalization classes retained their 1xxxx numbers. From about the 1970s, the D prefixes were omitted.

Further changes came with the introduction of British Railways' computerized vehicle-tracking system TOPS (Total Operation Processing System), in 1974. Each class of locomotive was given a two-digit number followed by a three-digit number for each locomotive. Initially, there was a gap between the first two digits and the last three, but this disappeared with the 'business liveries' in the 1980s.

For example, a 350hp diesel shunter built at Derby in January 1954 was first numbered 13059. It was renumbered D3059 in May 1958 and 08046 in July 1974, 08 being the class number and this one being the forty-sixth of the class, a number of the earlier ones having already been withdrawn.

As the TOPS numbers are familiar to most modellers, diesel locos are described in TOPS class order. Only those classes that ran on the LM Region and for which models are available are described.

British Railways Diesel Locomotives were initially painted unlined black but this was replaced by Dark Middle Chrome Green in the 1950s and all the Modernisation Plan diesels were painted green. A design panel was appointed to advise on the external appearance of the new locomotives. Livery variants were designed for each class of locomotive, to enhance their appearance, with light green or grey additions to the dark green livery. Initially, buffer beams were painted in the traditional railway red but, during the 1960s, yellow panels began to appear on locomotive ends to make them more visible. These were followed by full yellow ends.

The British Railways Board launched its new corporate image in 1964. The carefully selected Design Panel liveries were replaced by plain Rail Blue, with overall yellow ends, white numerals and the Double Arrow symbol. During the 1980s, new liveries began to appear as the railways moved towards a system of individual businesses. Freight locomotives were painted grey and Inter-City locomotives dark grey above the waist and white below, with a red stripe below the waist. The red, white and blue stripes of Network Southeast arrived in 1986, two years before the Regions disappeared. These liveries developed into the full sectorization liveries of the 1988–94 period, by

which time the London Midland Region had ceased to exist.

SOUTHERN REGION DIESEL ELECTRIC ICO-COIS 10201–10203

10201/2 were built at Ashford in 1950/51 and 10203 at Brighton in 1954. They had the same English Electric engine as 10000 and 10001, but rated at 1,750hp (10201/2) and 2,000hp (10203). As the Southern required a lower axle load than the LMS, they had an additional carrying axle at the outer end of each bogie.

They were used initially on the Waterloo–Exeter and Waterloo–Bournemouth routes, where they were joined in 1953 by the two LMR locos. All five were transferred to Camden in 1955 for use on the West Coast Main Line but they were in fact used mainly on outer suburban trains. Livery was black but they were repainted green when transferred to the LM Region. They were withdrawn at the end of 1963.

An OO gauge model has been announced by Kernow Model Railways.

BRITISH RAILWAYS CLASS 03 BR 204HP 0-6-0 DIESEL MECHANICAL SHUNTER

230 locos were built at Swindon (11187–11121, later D2000–D2024, D2025–D2043, D2114–D2199, D2370–D2384) and Doncaster (D2044–D2113, D2385–D2399) from 1957 to 1961 (TOPS 03004–03399). The three-figure number was the same last three figures of the D2xxx number.

Only D2198/9 and D2372–D2396 were allocated new to the LM Region, used for light shunting at a variety of locations. They were withdrawn between 1968 and 1972 without receiving TOPS numbers. Many are preserved.

Ready-to-run models are available from Bachmann for OO gauge, Graham Farish for N gauge and Heljan for O gauge.

DREWRY CAR CO. CLASS 04 204HP 0-6-0 DIESEL MECHANICAL SHUNTER

142 locos were built by Drewry Car Co. (between

11100–11229, later D2200–D2259, and D2260–D2341) between 1952 and 1962. None was allocated new to the LM Region but about twenty-five were transferred later for light shunting. They were withdrawn between 1968 and 1970. Although the class number 04 was issued, none received TOPS numbers. A number are preserved.

Mainline produced an OO gauge model, subsequently produced by Bachmann, but it is not currently available. Graham Farish produce an N gauge model.

HUNSLET ENGINE CO. CLASS 05 204HP 0-6-0 DIESEL MECHANICAL SHUNTER

Sixty-nine locos were built by Hunslet Engine Co. (11136–11176, later D2500–D2573 and D2574–D2618) between 1955 and 1961. None was allocated new to the LM Region but twenty-six were transferred later for light shunting work. They were withdrawn in 1967–68. Only D2553, transferred to the Isle of Wight, carried its TOPS number 05001. Four are preserved.

Heljan produce models for OO and O gauge.

BRITISH RAILWAYS CLASS 08 350HP 0-6-0 DIESEL ELECTRIC SHUNTER

The Class 08 was a development of the English Electric/LMS diesel shunter. Between 1952 and 1962, 1,193 were built at Derby, Darlington, Doncaster, Crewe and Horwich. They were numbered 13000–13357 (later D3000–D3357), D3358–D3362, 13363–13366 (later D3363–D3366) and D3367–D4192. By the time TOPS numbers were issued, some had been withdrawn and the survivors became 08001–08958. Some were re-geared to run at 27mph and these were classified 09. About 230 were allocated new to the LM Region for shunting work at all major centres.

In 2017, there were still sixty-eight 08s and three 09s registered to work on Network Rail and a larger number on heritage railways.

Hornby Dublo produced a model of an 08 and Tri-Ang produced an inside-framed version in the 1960s. Both Bachmann and Hornby now produce excellent OO gauge models of 08s and the old Tri-Ang inside-framed monstrosity is still available in Hornby's Railroad range. Graham Farish produce an N gauge model and Dapol an O gauge one.

BR Standard Class 08 350hp diesel electric shunter 08842. It is shunting a BG and Post Office vans in the red livery at Derby on 15 August 1990.

ENGLISH ELECTRIC CLASS 20
1,000HP DIESEL ELECTRIC BO-BO

The Class 20, built at EECo's Vulcan Foundry or by Robert Stephenson & Hawthorn with 1,000hp engine and electrical equipment by English Electric, was the first of the Modernisation Plan types to go into production. D8000–D8019 were built in 1957/8, and D8020–D8199 and D8300–D8327 between 1959 and 1968. They became TOPS 20001–20227, generally retaining the three-figure loco number, although D8000 became 20050, D8050 became 20128, D8128 became 20228 and D8300–D8327 became 20200–20227. Initial livery was green with a grey roof.

The first LM Region allocation was D8000–D8019 to East London (Bow), D8134–8136 to Birmingham and D8144–D8199 to Nottingham. Later, the Class 20s worked widely across the Region. Latterly, they generally worked as coupled pairs, with cabs outward, which could be driven by one man. Due to the poor lookout along the engine casing, they had to be double-manned when working singly. Their work was always predominantly short-distance goods work, including works trains, with occasional passenger work in the summer, when train heating was not required. Withdrawal started in 1976 but twenty-five were still registered to run on Network Rail in 2017 and rather more on heritage railways.

Hornby Dublo produced a model of a Class 20 in the 1950s and Lima produced an OO gauge one in 1985, an updated version of which is currently available from Hornby. Bachmann also produce OO gauge models of the Class 20 and the Class 20/3 variant, with modified ends and larger fuel tanks. Graham Farish produce a Class 20 for N gauge and Heljan one for O gauge.

BRITISH RAILWAYS CLASS 24
1,160HP DIESEL ELECTRIC BO-BO

The 151 Class 24 Bo-Bos D5000-D5150 were built at Derby, Crewe and Darlington with Sulzer engines and BTH (British Thompson Houston) electrical

Derby/Sulzer 1,160hp type 2 Bo-Bo D5025 (later Class 24) leaving Linslade tunnel on the 3.16pm Bletchley–Euston train on 27 July 1963. The train is composed of six or seven LMS Period 3 non-corridor suburban carriages.

Derby/Sulzer 1,250hp type 2 Bo-Bo 25067 arriving at Spondon on the 07.30 Saturday-only train from Nottingham to Llandudno in 1977. With 1,250hp for nine Mark 1s, progress was somewhat pedestrian. Note the Midland Railway-style platform fencing on the Up platform.

equipment between 1958 and 1961. D5000–D5113 were built with headcode discs, D5114–D5150 with headcode boxes on the cab roof and all had end gangway doors. They were renumbered between 24001 and 24150 in 1973–74; some had already been withdrawn and D5000 became 24005. Initial livery was green with a grey roof and a narrow grey stripe at the solebar.

D5000–D5019 and D5133–D5147 were allocated new to the LM Region at Crewe, Longsight and Willesden and were later joined by more. In the 1970s, Crewe had about forty. They were initially used on passenger and goods work but later were generally on goods work. Due to the elimination of most local goods trains, they were withdrawn between 1967 and 1980. 24061 was transferred to the Research Division and others were retained for train pre-heating. Four are preserved.

Bachmann produce OO gauge Class 24 models with both headcode arrangements and Sutton's Locomotive Works also produce the earlier version. The earlier version is available for N gauge from Graham Farish.

BRITISH RAILWAYS CLASS 25 1,250HP DIESEL ELECTRIC BO-BO

The Class 25 was a development of Class 24 with

an uprated Sulzer engine and electrical equipment by AEI (Associated Electrical Industries), which had taken over BTH. Numbers were D5151–D5299 and D7500–D7677. They were built by BR at Darlington and Derby and by Beyer Peacock (D7624–D7659). There were two main types of Class 25. D5151–D5232 and D7568–D7597, built between 1961 and 1963, had air-intake grilles in the bodyside and end gangway doors, and were painted in plain dark green with a grey solebar stripe. D5233–D5299, D7500–D7677 and D7598–D7677, built between 1963 and 1966, had the air-intake grilles above the cantrail and no end gangways and were painted dark green with a wide light green band between the solebar and the waist. D7660–D7677 were painted blue from new. They were renumbered 25001–25327 in numerical order, but with a few gaps due to early withdrawals.

Initial allocation to the LM Region was D5183–D5299, D7500–D7597 and D7650–D7677, mainly to Cricklewood, Nottingham and Toton, although D7670–7671 went to the Western section. The main use of Class 25s was for goods traffic on ex-Midland lines, with some passenger train operation. They were withdrawn between 1975 and 1987 and nine are preserved.

Bachmann produce OO gauge models of both

types of Class 25. The earlier version is produced for N gauge by Graham Farish and for O gauge by Heljan.

BIRMINGHAM RC&W CLASS 27 1,250HP DIESEL ELECTRIC BO-BO

The Class 27 was the Birmingham Carriage & Wagon Co.'s equivalent to the Class 25, with 1,250hp Sulzer engine and GEC (General Electric Co.) electrical equipment. D5374–D5414 were built in 1961–62, with D5379–D5415 being allocated to the LM Region at Cricklewood for goods and passenger work. However, all the 27s were moved to Scotland in 1967–68, together with the lower-powered Class 26, none of which had operated on the LM Region. Livery was dark green with a grey roof and narrow waist band. They never ran on the LM Region in blue livery or with 27xxx numbers.

Eight are preserved and Heljan produce a model for OO gauge and Dapol one for N gauge.

METROPOLITAN VICKERS CLASS 28 1,200HP DIESEL ELECTRIC CO-BO

Locomotives D5700–D5719 were built by Metropolitan Vickers with Crossley 2-stroke 1,200hp engines and Metro Vic Electrical Equipment in 1958–59. All were allocated to the LM Region at Derby and operated passenger and goods services over the Midland main line. Livery was dark green with a grey roof and grey band above the solebar.

The Crossley engine proved to be totally unsuited to railway work. The locomotives were moved to the North West and were withdrawn in 1967–68 without carrying their 28xxx numbers or blue livery. D5705 was transferred to the Research Division and is preserved.

Hornby Dublo produced a model in the 1960s and a much better OO gauge one is currently available from Heljan.

BRUSH CLASS 31 1,470HP DIESEL ELECTRIC A1A-A1A

Locomotives D5500–D5519 were built by Brush with 1,250hp Mirrlees engines and Brush electrical equipment in 1957–58. They were followed by D5520–D5699 and D5800–D5862, with 1,365hp engines, in 1959–62. All were initially allocated to the Eastern Region. Initial livery was dark green with a grey roof and white waist and solebar bands. In this state, they would have run on the LM Region only on incoming Eastern Region trains.

The Mirrlees engines were later found to be unsuited to rail traction and were replaced by

Two Metropolitan Vickers Co-Bo diesels ready to leave St Pancras on the 1.25pm to Manchester in June 1960, with an LNER Thompson coach in crimson and cream at the front of the train.

Class 31 Brush Type 2 A1A-A1A No. 31242 displays the Railfreight Grey livery with a red skirt at Crewe on 30 May 1989.

English Electric 1,470hp engines in 1965–68. D5520–D557/19 had a non-standard control system and were renumbered 31018, 31001–19. The others were renumbered 31101–31329 and 31401–31410, in original numerical order but with the 31/4s, with electric train supply, interspersed. There were ultimately sixty-nine ETS-equipped 31/4s.

31s began to appear on the LM Region in the 1970s, by which time they would all have been blue. Some later carried the grey freight livery. Withdrawal started in 1975; fifteen were still registered to run on Network Rail in 2017, but none in 2018. There are a number on heritage railways.

An excellent OO gauge model of a Class 31 was the first locomotive model produced by Airfix when it moved into model railways in the late 1970s. Lima later also produced a Class 31, the successor of which is still available in Hornby's Railroad range. A new Class 31 from Hornby appeared in 2005, but is not in the current catalogue. Graham Farish produce a Class 31 for N gauge and Heljan one for O gauge.

ENGLISH ELECTRIC CLASS 37 1,750HP DIESEL ELECTRIC CO-CO

A total of 309 locomotives (D6700–D6999 and D6600–D6608) were built by English Electric (Vulcan Foundry) and Robert Stephenson & Hawthorn, with English Electric 1,750hp engines and electrical equipment, between 1960 and 1965. None was initially allocated to the LM Region but would have worked in it, mainly on freight trains, from the Eastern or Western Regions. The LM Region did receive some later, after they were renumbered, with D6701 to D6608 becoming 37001 to 37308, in order. D6700 became 37119, D6819 became 37283 and D6983 was an early withdrawal. There were many variants and later renumberings. Initial livery was plain dark green. About seventy were registered to run on Network Rail in 2017.

An OO gauge model was produced by Lima in the 1980s, which is still available in Hornby's Railroad Range. Class 37 models for OO gauge are also available from Bachmann and VI Trains. Graham Farish produce an N gauge one and Heljan an O gauge.

ENGLISH ELECTRIC CLASS 40 2,000HP DIESEL ELECTRIC 1CO-CO1

The English Electric Class 40 was developed from the Southern Region prototype locomotives 10201–10203. D200–D399 were built between 1958 and 1962 by English Electric (Vulcan Foundry) and Robert Stephenson & Hawthorn, with English Electric 2,000hp engines and electrical equipment. Initial LM Region allocation was D210–D236, D267–D269, D287–D344 and D369–D384. They were all allocated to the West Coast Main Line and worked most express services until electrification took over in stages, after which they were more widely used on goods and passenger work. Initial livery was dark green with a grey roof and a white cantrail stripe.

D200 was renumbered 40122 and D201–D321, D323–D399 became 40001–40121, 40123–40199. D210–D225 and D227–D235 carried the names of passenger liners, mostly Cunard Line, which had used Liverpool docks. D322 was withdrawn in 1967 and the others between 1976 and 1988. Seven are preserved.

An OO gauge Class 40 model was produced by Lima in the 1990s and its successor was in Hornby's Railroad range, but is not in the current catalogue. Bachmann also produce a Class 40 model for O gauge, Graham Farish for N gauge and Heljan for O gauge.

BRITISH RAILWAYS CLASS 44, 45 AND 46 DIESEL ELECTRIC 1CO-CO1

Classes 44, 45 and 46 were similar to the 40s but were built in British Railways workshops. They had Sulzer engines and electrical equipment by Crompton Parkinson (Class 44 and 45) and Brush (Class 46). They were numbered in a single series from D1 to D193. Initial livery was dark green with a grey band above the solebar.

English Electric Type 4 1Co-Co1 (later Class 40) No. D214 leaving Linslade tunnel on the Up Ulster express from Liverpool on 27 July 1963. D214 is an early Class 40 with folding headcode discs.

45122, fitted to provide electric power to the train, passing Duffield on the 10.54 Hull–Cardiff on 26 May 1985. The train consists of Mark 2 pressure-ventilated carriages, with Mark 1 BG and buffet car.

D1 to D10 were built at Derby in 1959 with 2,300hp engines. They were initially allocated to Camden for West Coast express work but moved later to the East Midlands for freight work. They were renumbered 44001–44010 and were withdrawn between 1976 and 1980. 44004 and 44008 are preserved.

D11 to D137 were built at Derby and Crewe in 1960–62, with 2,500hp engines. D11/12 and D68–77 were initially allocated to the West Coast Main Line, and all the rest to the Midland Main Line, although some went later to the Eastern Region. Fifty were modified to provide electrical train supply in 1973–75. They were renumbered 45001–45077 and 45101–45150 (ETS locos) in order of renumbering, so with no correlation between original and new numbers. 45/1s would then have been used mainly for passenger work and 45/0s on goods. They were used on Midland Main Line, cross-country and trans-Pennine trains. The 45s were withdrawn between 1980 and 1988.

D138–D193 were built at Derby in 1961–63, with 2,500hp Sulzer engines and Brush electrical equipment. D138–D165 were initially allocated to Derby and D166 to D193 to the North Eastern Region; some went later to the Western Region. They were not modified to provide electric train supply and were renumbered 46001–46056 in the order of the original numbers. They worked both passenger and goods trains, in particular on cross-country routes, but could not work with air-conditioned stock. The 46s were withdrawn between 1978 and 1984, but four were transferred to the Research Division and one is preserved.

An OO gauge model of a 45 or 46 was produced by Mainline in the 1990s and its successor is still available, in a number of varieties, from Bachmann.

47409 Rail Riders passing Bedford on a special train of newly painted Post Office vans on 20 September 1986. 47409 is in InterCity livery and the vans are in a unique livery variant, in which the 'all-red' specification was extended to the roofs.

For N gauge, Graham Farish produce models of all three classes, 44, 45 and 46, while Heljan produce a 45 for O gauge.

BRUSH CLASS 47 2,580HP DIESEL ELECTRIC CO-CO

D1500–D1999 and D1100–D1111 were built by Brush or by BR at Crewe between 1962 and 1968. They used the same power equipment as Class 46, but with the engine uprated to 2,750hp, and with a more compact Co-Co wheel arrangement. Following various problems, the engines were derated to 2,580hp. Most went initially to the Eastern and Western Regions, with the LM Region receiving D1616–D1635 in 1964, the Midland lines D1807–D1861 in 1965, and the Western lines D1939–D1961 in 1967. Initial livery was dark green with a lime green band between solebar and waist.

The 47s were renumbered 47000–47381 and 47401–47528, the latter being fitted with electric train supply. There were numerous later renumberings as different variants were produced. Some 47s carried Intercity, Freight or Network Southeast liveries a few years before the business sectors had taken over operations from the Regions. 47s were likely to turn up on any main lines, on passenger or goods work. In 2017, there were still about fifty 47s

running on Network Rail, plus about thirty that have been re-equipped with General Motors engines and reclassified Class 57.

Hornby and Lima produced OO gauge Class 47 models in the 1980s and the Lima model is still available in Hornby's Railroad range. OO gauge Class 47s are also available from Bachmann, Heljan and VI Trains. Graham Farish produce a 47 for N gauge and Heljan one for O gauge.

ENGLISH ELECTRIC CLASS 50 2,700HP DIESEL ELECTRIC CO-COS

D400–D499 were built by English Electric at Vulcan Foundry in 1967–68 as the production version of the prototype DP2, and were initially leased to British Railways from English Electric. All were initially allocated to the LM and Scottish Regions, working expresses between Crewe and Glasgow, frequently in pairs. When electrification to Glasgow was completed, in 1975, they were transferred to the Western Region. They were all new in Rail Blue livery. D400 became 50050 and D401–D449 became 50001–50049.

The 50s were all withdrawn by the early 1990s, but five preserved examples were still registered to run on Network Rail in 2017. Hornby produced an OO gauge model in 2004, which is currently available, and Dapol produce one for N gauge.

BRUSH CLASS 56 3,250HP DIESEL ELECTRIC CO-CO

56001–56135 were built by Brush Traction, as main contractor, during 1976. They had Ruston-Paxman 3,250hp engines and Brush electrical equipment, but locomotive building was sub-contracted to Electroputere of Romania (56001–56030), BREL Doncaster (56031–56115) and BREL Crewe (56116–56135).

56031–56072 were allocated to Toton (LM Region), while the others went to the Eastern Region. They were all for use on 'merry-go-round' coal traffic. They did work other air-braked goods traffic, but were not fitted to work vacuum-braked trains. Initial livery was Rail Blue with a small Double Arrow logo, but later locos appeared with a large Double Arrow.

Most of the 56s were withdrawn in the 2000s as EWS introduced its preferred Class 66s, although in 2017 about thirty were still listed for running on Network rail.

Hornby produce an OO gauge model for a Class 56 and Dapol one for N gauge.

BREL CLASS 58 3,300HP DIESEL ELECTRIC CO-CO

British Rail Engineering Ltd built 58001–58050 at Doncaster in 1983–87, with Ruston-Paxman 3,300hp engines and Brush electrical equipment. In the hope of getting export orders, they were built like American locos, with removable side panels to the equipment compartments. They were all allocated to Toton (LM Region) for coal traffic, although some did appear on other air-braked traffic. Initial livery was Railfreight Grey with large Double Arrow logo, but 58050 was new in the Railfreight Sector Double Grey with coal sector logos.

Generally superseded by Class 66s by 2002, thirty-six 58s were sold for use in France or Spain. None was registered for running on Network Rail in 2017, although two are on heritage railways. Hornby produced an OO gauge model of a 58 in

56018, in Railfreight Grey with coal sector markings, passing Stenson junction on a southbound train of empty HEA coal hoppers livery, mainly in Railfreight Red, on 27 August 1991.

58026, in Railfreight Grey with coal sector markings, passing Derby station on a train of empty HAA 'merry-go-round' coal wagons on 12 September 1990.

the 1990s and one is currently available from Heljan. An N gauge model is produced by Dapol.

CLASS 43 HIGH-SPEED TRAIN POWER CARS

British Railways' High-Speed Train was developed in the 1970s when it was determined that a maximum speed of 125mph (200km/h) was necessary for the railways to compete with road transport and airlines for inter-city traffic. Two prototype power cars 41000 and 41001 were built at Crewe in 1972, with Paxman 2,250hp engines and Brush electrical equipment, together with a prototype set of Mark 3 carriages built at Derby, initially designed to operate either between two HST power cars or in loco-hauled trains.

After initial testing, during which a speed of 143mph (almost 230km/h) was reached, the HST was allocated to the Eastern Region to operate the North Briton Leeds–Edinburgh service. As it happened, the Trades Unions saw the HST as a bargaining tool for getting improved conditions, and the train ran empty over the route, achieving 125mph between York and Darlington.

253.025 (43050+43051) at Nottingham on the 12.15 St Pancras– Sheffield on 10 October 1982.

To reduce weight and cost, it was then decided that the production HSTs should be fitted with 3-phase AC train supply, while the loco-hauled Mark 3 carriages would have the standard DC supply. The prototype carriages and one power car were rebuilt for 3-phase supply and were transferred to the Western Region, which was going to receive the first production HSTs. The train was classified as a unit train, 252.001, and entered service on 14 May 1975 between Bristol and Paddington.

The production HSTs were initially seen as fixed formation unit trains classified 253 (Western Region 7-car sets) and 254 (Eastern Region 8-car sets). Although they were not allocated to the LM Region, initial testing of all sets took place on the LM Region.

Following the first deliveries to the Western Region, the second batch went to the Eastern and the third batch to cross-country services, which ran over the LM Region. A redeployment of units led to an allocation to the Midland Main Line between St Pancras and Sheffield from 1982.

ELECTRIC LOCOMOTIVES

Although a number of local electrification schemes were introduced by the LMS and its predecessors, these were all suburban passenger services operated by electric multiple, which are described in the section on carriages.

CLASS 76 1,360HP 1,500V DC BO-BO ELECTRIC LOCOMOTIVES

In 1941, the LNER built a single locomotive No. 6701, with Metropolitan Vickers electrical equipment. It was trialled on the Manchester–Altrincham line and loaned to the Netherlands Railways (NS) between 1946 and 1952, to gain operating experience, pending completion of the Manchester–Sheffield–Wath electrification. It was numbered 6000 in 1946, later becoming BR 26000. After the nationalization, the western end of the ex-LNER Manchester-Sheffield line became part of the LM Region.

Thirty similar locos were built at Gorton in 1950–51, classified EM1 and numbered 26001–26030. They were used mainly in pairs on the MSW coal traffic but with some passenger work, for which fourteen were fitted with boilers. Initial livery was black with red lining, later lined green. They were repainted Rail Blue from 1966. The passenger service over the line was taken off in 1970 and withdrawal of the EM1s started. The survivors were renumbered 76001–4, 76006–16, 76018 and 76020–30.

The 76s were withdrawn between 1970 and 1981,

EM1 (Later Class 76) Bo-Bo 26038 at Godley junction on empty coal wagons for Wath, with a wooden ex-private owner wagon at the front, whilst another EM1 approaches on loaded coal wagons on 26 April 1960. Note the heavy portal structures required for the 1,500V DC contact wire.

when the line was closed, except for a short section at the Manchester end, which was retained for a passenger service. 26020 is preserved.

Trix produced an OO gauge model in the 1960s and Heljan now produce a much better one, available from Olivia's Trains.

CLASS 77 2,400HP 1,500V DC CO-CO ELECTRIC LOCOMOTIVES

Class EM2 locos 27000–27006 were built in 1953–54 at Gorton and Dukinfield, with Metropolitan Vickers electrical equipment, for Manchester–Sheffield passenger services. Livery was black with red lining, later lined green, and Rail Blue from 1966. Although classified 77, they were never renumbered. In 1968, they were sold to the Netherlands Railways (NS) and renumbered 1501–1506, with 27005 being dismantled for spares.

The last four were withdrawn by the NS in 1986, and 1502 and 1505 returned to Britain for preservation. An OO gauge model was produced by Tri-Ang in the 1960s and one is currently available from Heljan, through Olivia's Trains.

CLASS 81 TO 85 25KV AC BO-BO ELECTRIC LOCOMOTIVES

The Class 81 to 85 locomotives, originally classified AL1 to AL5, were built between 1959 and 1964 for the first stages of the West Coast electrification. All had a continuous rating of about 3,200hp and a maximum speed of 100mph. All had similar styling, with a sloping cab front and were initially painted Electric Blue with white cab roofs and window surrounds, stainless-steel numerals on the cab sides and cast alloy BR crests in the centre of the bodyside. They were all built with two pantographs but, by about 1970, they had only one pantograph, along with Rail Blue livery with yellow ends and various other modifications.

Class AL1 locos E3001–23 and E3096/97 were built by Birmingham RC&W Co. with AEI(BTH) electrical equipment in 1959–64. E3002/9/19 were withdrawn early but the others were numbered 81001–81022 in 1973/4. Most were based latterly in Scotland and were withdrawn between 1984 and 1992.

Class AL2 locos E3046–55 were built by Beyer Peacock with Metropolitan Vickers electrical equipment in 1960–62. E3046 and E3055 were withdrawn early but the others were renumbered 82001–82008 in 1974. They were withdrawn between 1983 and 1987.

Class AL3 locos E3024–35, E3303/4 and E3100 were built in 1960–62 by English Electric at Vulcan

Class AL1 (later Class 81) BRC&W/ AEI Bo-Bo locomotive E3012 at Euston on 19 March 1966 in the Electric Blue livery, with the addition of a yellow panel.

Foundry, with English Electric electrical equipment. E3303/4 were originally geared for a maximum speed of 80mph and were renumbered E3098/9 when re-geared for 100mph in 1962. The 83s had persistent problems with their mercury arc rectifiers and spent much time in store. E3100 had experimental solid-state rectifiers, which later became standard after the whole class were rebuilt at Doncaster in 1971.

They were renumbered 83001–83015 in 1973/3 and were withdrawn between 1977 and 1980, with 83015 lasting to 1989.

Class AL4 locos E3036–45 were built in 1960–61 by The North British Loco Co., with General Electric electrical equipment. Like the AL3s, they had persistent rectifier problems until rebuilt at Doncaster in 1971. They were renumbered 84001–84010 in 1974. They were withdrawn between 1977 and 1980 and 84001 was chosen for preservation by the National Railway Museum.

Class AL5 locos E3056–95 were built in 1961–64 by BR at Doncaster, with AEI(BTH) electrical equip-ment, similar to that in the AL1s but with solid-state rectifiers. They were renumbered 85001–85040 in 1973–75. Withdrawal started in 1983 but some

were still running in the 1990s, mainly on goods work.

Bachmann produce an OO gauge model.

CLASS 86 25KV AC BO-BO ELECTRIC LOCOMOTIVES

Following experience with the AL1 to AL5 classes, 100 Class AL6 locos were built at Doncaster (E3101–E3140) and Vulcan Foundry (E3141–E3200) in 1965/6 with AEI Electrical equipment with a con-tinuous rating of 4,040hp. They were ready for the completion of the West Coast electrification into Euston. The design was similar to the earlier locos but with two minor visual differences, and one important technical change. The cab front was now vertical below the waist, with only the windscreen angled and livery was Rail Blue, still with the cast BR crest on the first locos; cast Double Arrow logos appeared later.

While Class AL1–AL5 had fully suspended traction motors, the AL6s were built with nose-suspended traction motors. It was not long before the Civil Engineer began to complain about what the AL6s were doing to his track – and the drivers were not too happy either. This led to a number

An 86/4 in InterCity livery approaching Stowe Hill tunnel on the 13.10 Euston–Wolverhampton, composed of Mark 2 air-conditioned carriages, on 17 March 1989.

of modifications with Class 87 bogies (Class 86/1), flexicoil suspension (Class 86/2) and resilient wheels (Class 86/3). Unmodified 86/0 locos were limited to 80mph and confined to goods work.

The AL6s were renumbered with 86xxx TOPS numbers in 1973, the third numeral indicating the sub class of each loco and the last two numerals bearing no relationship to that of the original E31xx number. Further renumbering occurred later.

OO gauge models of Class 86s are available from Hornby and Heljan and an N gauge one from Dapol.

CLASS 87 25KV AC BO-BO ELECTRIC LOCOMOTIVES

Class 87 locos 87001–87035 and 87101 were built at Crewe with GEC electrical equipment, with a continuous rating of 5,000hp, in 1973–75, ready for the extension of the West Coast electrification to Glasgow. They used the flexicoil suspension and bogies that were developed for the 86/1s. In a minor visual change from Classes 81–86, there were now only two cab windscreens in place of three. 87101 was equipped with thyristor power control.

Class 87 models are available for OO gauge from Hornby and for N gauge from Graham Farish.

CLASS 90 25KV AC BO-BO ELECTRIC LOCOMOTIVES

Class 90 locos 90001–90050 were built at Crewe, with GEC electrical equipment, in 1987–90. They were a development of 87101, with streamlined cabs, with a maximum speed of 110mph. 90001–90025 were delivered in InterCity livery and some operated briefly on the LM Region, before it disappeared. 90026–90050 went to the new freight companies.

Class 90 models are available for OO gauge from Bachmann and for N gauge from Graham Farish.

A Class 87 at Watford on an Up express composed of Mark 2 air-conditioned carriages in blue and grey livery on 23 February 1975.

The first Class 90 electric locos entered service as the LM Region was disappearing. 90010 arriving at Lancaster on the 10.30 Euston–Glasgow on 30 May 1989. Note the head-span overhead line support system.

MAKERS' PROTOTYPES

Much to the surprise of passengers when they disembarked from the ferry from the Isle of Man in Liverpool in summer 1958, a big light blue diesel was at the head of the connecting train. The Manxman was sitting in Lime Street terminus, and the locomotive rostered to haul it was the prototype Deltic. This 3,300bhp Co-Co had been built speculatively by English Electric in 1955, with an eye on both the British and American markets. Thus, each cab front sported a large, deep nose and a protuberance that might, in the USA, have contained a large headlamp (although it did not in the UK).

Deltic was the most powerful diesel locomotive in the UK at the time, and the first to be designed to run at 100mph. It was powered by two Napier diesel engines, each of which had three crankshafts being driven by thirty-six pistons, working as opposed pistons in eighteen long cylinders arranged in a 'delta' (or triangular) formation – hence its name. Electrically, the locomotive was a conventional diesel electric with six axle-hung traction motors.

A return run from Liverpool to London was a sensible way of proving the locomotive in service; Liverpool was a convenient starting point for the English Electric engineers, based at Preston, who needed to accompany it during its early trials. In the end, however, it was the three Regions running the East Coast Main Line that recognized the potential of the design. Twenty-two Deltics were ordered

for the ECML in 1959. The prototype was retired in 1961 and spent three decades on display in the Science Museum in London. It is now in the hands of the National Railway Museum and has recently been on display at the NRM's Shildon museum.

A OO scale model of Deltic has been produced by Bachmann, with an N gauge one available from Graham Farish. Back in the 1960s, Rosebud Kitmaster produced a very good OO scale non-motored plastic kit of it, which is still available under the Dapol banner.

Funnily enough, the next time the same group of passengers came home from the Isle of Man, in 1962, the Manxman express to London had another prototype diesel at its head. This time it was DP2, an English Electric Co-Co design for the more powerful end of the Type 4 market, which was to be dominated by the Brush Type 4s (47s). DP2 looked like a production Deltic (the D9000 series), having a very similar body shape, and was running with the same basic designs of bogies and traction motors. However, inside the body it was quite different. It had one large 16-cylinder turbocharged and intercooled diesel engine developing up to 2,700bhp. Technically, it was a more powerful and lighter-weight version of the English Electric Type 4 (Class 40). DP2 ended up on the ECML on mixed-traffic working, until it was damaged in a collision with some derailed cement wagons. The damage precipitated its withdrawal.

BR, however, had noted DP2's successful operation and ordered fifty Class 50 Co-Cos with the

The prototype English Electric Co-Co Deltic stands at the head of the Up Manxman express at Liverpool Lime Street in summer 1958.

same traction equipment and a different body shape. The control system was electronic this time and this would prove to be a source of much unreliability in service. The 50s were commonly seen on the West Coast Main Line, often in pairs, until electrification to Carlisle and Glasgow ousted them. They were then moved to the Western Region.

A model of DP2 in OO scale was produced in 2011 by Heljan, and Dapol was reported as developing one, too.

The other three 'big Type 4' prototypes, Lion, Falcon and Kestrel, were not used for any length of time on the LM Region and so are not appropriate for inclusion here.

EARLY ODDITIES

Much earlier, of course, were the Fell diesel and also No. 10800, referred to in the previous chapter. The Fell was a 1952 attempt to prove that diesel mechanical transmission could match the output of a 2,000bhp diesel electric. Numbered by BR as 10100, it was originally laid out as a 2D2 (4-8-4 in Whyte notation).

A1 Models once produced a OO scale kit that made a neat representation of 10100, but no one to date has produced a ready-to-run version.

10800 was a conventional Bo-Bo hood unit diesel electric, also built by BR Derby Works, of 800bhp. This worked out of Derby for a time, and also on the Southern Region from 1952 to 1954. It was then set aside in 1958 until Brush Traction took it over in 1961/2 for fitting experimental electronic traction control. It was withdrawn in 1968 and scrapped in 1972.

Dave Alexander has produced a metal kit for 10800 in OO scale.

Four years later, on 1 September 1962, another product of English Electric heads the Manxman. This time, it is the 2,700bhp Co-Co DP2, photographed during the short stop at Rugby en route to London Euston.

CHAPTER FOUR

PASSENGER ROLLING STOCK

This chapter describes the passenger carriages and non-passenger-carrying coaching stock (NPCCS) that ran on the London Midland Region of British Railways between 1948 and 1988, when the functions of the Regions passed to the business sectors, InterCity, Network South East and Regional Railways. Diesel and electric railcars and multiple units are also described. Ready-to-run OO gauge models are identified from *Model Rail* magazine's publication *Britain's Model Trains 2017*, although reference is also made to some previously available models and kits.

TRAIN FORMATIONS

The formation of each scheduled train that ran on the British railway system was laid down in Passenger Train Marshalling books. In 1948, most trains provided accommodation for first-class and third-class passengers, although some suburban and branch services were third-class only. There had once been a second class but this had disappeared before the formation of the LMS, although three classes remained on Continental railways. When the Continental railways abolished the third class, in 1958, British Railways third class became second class and has since become standard class.

For the modeller of the LM Region, Clive S. Carter's *LMS-LM Region Passenger Train Formations 1923–1983*, published by Ian Allan 1987, lists the formations of selected LM Region main-line trains over that particular period and also includes typical LMS and LM Region local and branch train formations. Until the 1960s, many main-line expresses included carriages for a number of destinations and some branch-line trains would have included a main-line through coach. With the introduction of diesel multiple units and the more intensive use of rolling stock, through-carriages and multi-portion

trains disappeared, as did the summer Saturday-only trains, formed of elderly carriages that only worked one journey per week.

Unlike passenger trains, parcels train formations tended to comprise a mixture of vehicles from all the BR Regions, in a variety of liveries and frequently very dirty. There had to be at least one guard's compartment in the train.

LIVERIES AND NUMBERS

At the start of 1948, all the London Midland Region's carriage stock would have carried LMS maroon livery. Many carriages looked somewhat careworn as a result of a lack of maintenance during the war. Carriages continued to be painted in LMS livery until late 1949, but the LMS lettering was omitted and the carriages received an M prefix to their previous LMS numbers.

In 1949, the first British Railways liveries were introduced. The red became a brighter crimson, also referred to as 'carmine'. On corridor carriages, the area between the windows was painted cream. There was a yellow/black/yellow line between the cream and lower crimson area and a yellow/black line between the cream and the crimson cantrail panel. Non-corridor carriages were painted in unlined crimson. Ends and underframes remained black and roofs grey.

Initially, the LMS carriage number was painted below the waist towards the left end of the carriage, with a regional prefix. The number was later moved to the right end, with regional prefix and a suffix. The prefix indicated the owning Region and the suffix the vehicle's origin. For example, M1234M would indicate a carriage of LMS origin allocated to the LM Region; E2345M was an LMS vehicle allocated to the Eastern Region; and M3456E was an LNER vehicle allocated to the London Midland

Region. British Railways standard carriages were numbered in a single series, each carriage having a regional prefix to indicate its allocation but no suffix. The regional prefixes were removed after the demise of the Regions, in 1988.

In 1956, British Railways adopted a carriage livery similar to the LMS Crimson Lake, but retaining the British Railways lining and lettering. This livery was applied to both corridor and non-corridor carriages. Initially, underframes and ends remained black, but, with changes to painting techniques, ends began to appear in the bodyside colour during the 1960s. The Southern Region began to paint all its carriages in the green, which had, until then, been used only on electric multiple units and the Western Region began to paint selected carriage sets, mainly BR standard Mark 1 vehicles, in chocolate and cream but reverted to the standard Crimson Lake after a few years. These liveries appeared on some through trains on to the London Midland Region. Another change in about 1960 was the painting of a yellow band in the cantrail panel above first-class compartments and a red band above catering facilities. The change from third to second class was invisible, as these classes were not indicated on the carriages.

The British Railways livery for diesel and electric multiple units was green. This was initially a darker version of the Southern's bright Malachite Green, but Locomotive Dark Green was used from the early 1960s and was also seen on many of the diesel multiple units in the 1950s.

When the British Rail corporate image was introduced, carriages began to appear in the corporate blue and grey livery. The experimental XP64 train was painted in blue and grey in 1964, followed by new Mark 2 carriages and repainting of existing carriages in 1966. Corridor carriages were Rail Blue with a light grey belt between the top and bottom of the windows, with a white line between the blue and grey areas. Lettering was white. Non-corridor carriages, most passenger-rated vans and multiple units were plain Rail Blue, although some gangwayed passenger brake vans were blue and grey, as were some DMU classes, which were built for longer-distance cross-country services.

A programme of internal refurbishment of some DMU classes started in the mid-1970s, with refurbished vehicles being painted white with a dark blue band below the waist. By the late 1970s, all refurbished DMUs were receiving the standard blue and grey livery. Passenger Transport Executives (PTEs) were introduced in major conurbations in the middle 1970s. Their main function was to operate the bus services but they also had some control over local rail services. PTEs were set up in the LM Region in the Greater Manchester, Merseyside and West Midlands areas, and in South and West Yorkshire in ex-LM Region areas. The PTE logos appeared on local trains, in addition to the BR Double Arrow, and PTE liveries began to replace the blue and grey.

Post Office sorting and stowage vans had generally been painted in the standard carriage livery of the operating railway, but with Royal Mail lettering on the side. The BR Mark 1 Post Office vans were painted Post Office Red until standard blue and grey came in. From 1986, Post Office vans and other vans allocated to postal trains began to appear in Post Office Red with two yellow stripes on the lower bodyside.

As full repaints occurred at approximately five-year intervals, with 'touching up and varnishing' at intermediate repairs, trains of mixed liveries would have been common throughout most of the duration of the LM Region.

LMS PASSENGER ROLLING STOCK

When the London Midland Region of British Railways was formed, in 1948, most of its rolling stock would have been built by the London Midland and Scottish Railway. There would have been some pre-grouping vehicles but these had gone by the late 1950s. During the British Railways period, numerous vehicles were transferred from one Region to another, with changes of regional boundaries.

PERIOD 1 CORRIDOR CARRIAGES

The first new corridor carriages built by the LMS

between 1923 and 1929 had timber bodies on steel underframes, with side doors to all compartments. Bodysides and ends were timber, with beading covering the panel joints, and roofs were timber, covered with canvas. Open saloon carriages, referred to by the LMS as vestibule carriages, had two windows to each bay of seats. In *The LMS Coach 1923–1957*, published by Ian Allan in 1969, Jenkinson and Essery coined the term 'Period 1' for this design, and the name quickly became generally accepted. Period 1 carriages would not have been formed into front-line express trains after about 1950, but would have appeared in local trains, specials and reliefs until about 1960.

Mainline introduced OO gauge models of the LMS Period 1 corridor brake third and composite in the 1980s, which were later produced by Bachmann but are not in the current catalogue.

PERIOD 2 AND 3 CORRIDOR CARRIAGES

From 1932 to 1947, LMS carriages still had timber-framed bodies on steel underframes, but the bodysides, ends and roofs were covered by steel sheeting. Access to corridor carriages was by doors in the end vestibules, although additional doors in the corridors were provided from 1945. Each pas-senger compartment and each seating bay in open carriages had a single large window with sliding ventilators above. This design is known as Period 3. There was a brief intermediate Period 2, during which some of the features of the Period 3 designs were applied to timber bodywork. Period 3 corridor carriages had generally disappeared from main-line expresses by 1960, but ran in secondary services and reliefs until the late 1960s. A number are preserved and run on heritage railways.

Airfix produced OO gauge models of a Period 3 corridor brake third and composite in the 1980s, which are currently produced in kit form by Dapol. The composite is particularly useful as it was a common vehicle in LM Region trains and is not otherwise available. Hornby also produced OO gauge models of a Period 3 corridor brake third and composite, but on a generic underframe, which was more GWR than anything else, as the composite was too short. They are still available in Hornby's Railroad range but are not recommended to serious modellers.

A Period 3 open third was produced in the 1990s by Replica Railways and later by Bachmann, but has not been available for some years. The open third was another very common vehicle in LM Region trains.

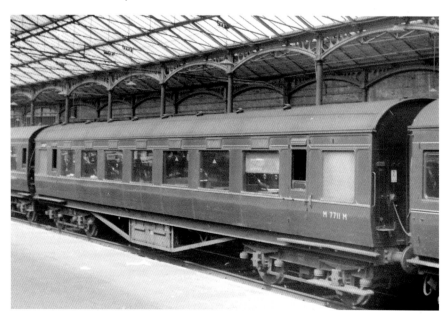

Period 2 Open Second M 7711 M at Euston in an excursion train on 9 June 1962. This had been built in 1930 with steel body panels but retaining the wood and canvas roof of the Period 1 designs.

LMS Period 3 brake third W 5814 M is no ordinary vehicle. First, its number indicates that it has been transferred to the Western Region, then the roof ducting shows that it is one of three brake thirds rebuilt in 1937 with pressure ventilation, for the Coronation Scot Euston–Glasgow high-speed service.

'Porthole' corridor composite M 24567 M at Swindon on 15 May 1964. The porthole composites were of all-steel construction with a different cross-section from the other carriages.

Dapol produced an OO gauge model of a Period 2 12-wheel dining car in the 1990s, which is now produced by Hornby. It rides a little high and has an unsightly cut-out in the underframe to allow it to go around train-set curves. With these faults dealt with, it fits in well with other models and is the only LMS catering vehicle available ready to run.

Hornby recently introduced a new range of OO gauge LMS Period 3 corridor brake third, corridor first, corridor third and gangwayed brake van and a Civil Engineer's Inspection saloon. An inspection saloon, with locomotive, was always likely to turn up anywhere on the system throughout the LM Region period and later.

For N gauge modellers, Graham Farish produce a range of Period 3 open third, composite, corridor third, corridor first, brake first, brake third, gangwayed brake van and inspection coach.

For many of the missing vehicles, Comet Kits are available, or Comet brass sides, which can be attached to a suitable ready-to-run model of a similar carriage of the same length. Some work will be required to cut away parts of the plastic bodyside, and rearrangement of the interior and roof details.

PORTHOLE CORRIDOR CARRIAGES

The final versions of Period 3 design incorporated round lavatory windows and are known as 'porthole' stock. They were all built in early British Railways days in 1948–50. The porthole composites were unusual in having all-steel bodies with a different cross-section. They had generally disappeared from main-line expresses by 1960 but ran in secondary services and reliefs until the late 1960s, and a few carried the blue and grey livery. A number are preserved on heritage railways, some carrying unauthentic LMS livery but looking good in it.

Bachmann produce a range of OO gauge porthole stock corridor carriages, corridor third, corridor first, corridor brake third, corridor brake first, and corridor composite.

LMS NON-CORRIDOR CARRIAGES

The LMS built a relatively small quantity of non-corridor lavatory carriages, to Period 1 and Period 2 standards, for secondary services on country lines, but, by 1950, these trains were more likely to be formed of older corridor carriages, although a few of the lavatory carriages survived to about 1960.

Airfix produced OO gauge models of a Period 2 lavatory composite and lavatory third in the 1980s, which are currently available in kit form from Dapol.

For purely suburban or branch-line use, the LMS built non-corridor carriages to Period 1, 2 and 3 standards until 1951. A variant on the non-corridor design was the push-pull trains operated on some country services, comprising a brake third, with a driver's position at the brake end, and a composite. Apart from the driver's cab, these were standard non-corridor carriages. A combination of branch-line closures and the introduction of DMUs in the late 1950s saw the end of non-corridor carriages, apart from a few purely suburban lines, by the early 1960s.

No strictly accurate model of an LMS Period 2 non-corridor carriage has been produced, but in the 1980s Graham Farish produced generic models of non-corridor and corridor brake third and third/composite, in both OO and N gauge, which can still be found on second-hand stalls. The non-corridor carriages are slightly short and narrow models of LMS Period 2 vehicles. The generic corridor carriages are based on Southern vehicles, so of no use to LM modellers.

Hornby have recently introduced OO gauge models of LMS Period 3 non-corridor composite, third and brake third. Maybe one day there will be a push-pull version of the brake third?

No ready-to-run model is available of LMS push-pull train carriages, but these were all derivatives of the standard non-corridor brake third and composite, with a driver's compartment in the brake end of the brake third. There are two LM Region push-pull trains on Famous Trains Model Railway's Chinley layout. One is rebuilt from Dapol lavatory coaches and the other from Graham Farish coaches. Neither is totally correct, as LMS push-pull carriages did not offer lavatory accommodation and the Farish ones are too short and narrow.

LMS Period 3 push-pull driving trailer brake second M 24454 M at Amlwch on 9 July 1964. Apart from the driving controls and end windows, the only difference from the standard brake second is the absence of the guard's-side look-out and a drop light in its place on the far side of the carriage.

A MODEL PUSH-PULL TRAIN

The Famous Trains model railway wanted a model steam push-pull train to run in and out of the bay platform at Chinley station, alternating with a DMU, to increase the interest for visitors.

However, the Famous Trains shop stocks Dapol plastic kits for LMS suburban non-corridor coaches. Two of these came in handy to make up a very convincing push-pull set. Finding a locomotive was less difficult. Bachmann has produced from time to time its model of an Ivatt Class 2 2-6-2T in push-pull and non-push-pull forms. One of these was obtained from Hattons – pre-owned as the push-pull model was out of production at the time when we needed the model.

We set about putting together the two Dapol carriage kits. One was a standard class compartment coach and the other was similar, but included a brake van. Both included central lavatory compartments, which the LM Region push-pull trains did not have. However, this was a small detail and not unduly concerning as most visitors would probably not notice it.

Before putting the kits together, we painted the inside compartment walls a light grey to vary the dark red interiors, and did the same for the guard's van area, which would soon include the driver's position. Externally, we repainted the carmine red coach bodies into later BR maroon and used a lining transfer (actually a Midland Railway one, but it looked OK) to line out the waist bands of the two carriages' sides. The driving cab front windows had to be drilled and filed out of the guard's van end on the kit. We drilled holes in the corners of the window positions, and filed out the plastic between them to cut away the window spaces. Glazing was cut to shape from a suitable clear plastic sheet (from a food packet window), and glued in place behind the front windows. All four carriage ends needed painting matt black because that was the BR style until the main works started using spray painting, around 1965–66, when a few maroon coaches received maroon ends.

We needed to add the rather prominent sun visors that the LMS or BR had fitted above the three front windows when the railway converted these existing suburban carriages for their push-pull role. A short strip of triangular-section plastic rod was cut into the three lengths, then the pieces glued in place above the end windows, and painted black. We painted semi-matt varnish over the bodysides and ends to secure the lining transfers and even out any differences in paint sheen.

Assembling the vehicles was simplicity itself. The body interiors fitted neatly into the body mouldings,

Famous Trains' first push-pull train runs into Chinley station propelled by Ivatt Class 2 2 6 2T 41221. The two coaches are from modified Dapol kits.

The driving trailer coach was repainted in maroon (the original was carmine red) and lined out from a Midland Railway transfer sheet. Acrylic matt varnish gives it its sheen.

as did the glazing mouldings, which had to be pressed out from the inside to fill the window spaces. The roofs clipped on to the tops of the glazing mouldings. No glue was necessary. The bogies just needed the wheelsets inserting and the pivots pushing into place into the holes in the body floors, where they again clipped into position. As we wanted our carriages to be closer-coupled than the OO scale manufacturers usually allow, with their over-long hook-and-bar couplings, we cut the backs off the two couplings of the non-driving coach, removed the hooks from these, and super-glued each shortened coupling bar unit on to the underside of the bogie moulding further back by about 3 to 4mm (see below). After some adjustment, the whole train coupled fairly tightly together, with the side buffers not quite touching each other. It all looked fine.

Famous Trains is very happy with its first push-pull train. We have since made another one from two old Graham Farish suburban coaches, with the driving cab end modified in exactly the same way. This train runs with a Bachmann-produced Lancashire & Yorkshire Railway 2-4-2T, some of which were allocated to depots on the Midland Division of the LM Region. This runs into our imaginary country terminus at Darley Green.

We now look forward to the eventual production of Bachmann's anticipated Midland Johnson 0-4-4T with push-pull gear, which we have on pre-order. That will enable us to have a standby locomotive for our two regular push-pull engines.

The cab end of the modified driving trailer coach shows the three windows that were drilled and knifed out of the end panel, and the three sun visors cut from triangular plastic rod.

The underside of the intermediate coach shows the repositioned coupling bar superglued to the coupling mounting on the bogie headstock. This enables the hook from the unaltered adjacent coach end to engage; the two sets of buffers run much closer together now, looking more realistic.

NON-PASSENGER-CARRYING COACHING STOCK (NPCCS)

All the British railway companies built vehicles that could run in passenger trains but did not include passenger accommodation. These included luggage and guard's brake vans, horseboxes, Post Office vans, milk vans and other specialized vehicles. Some goods wagons, fitted with vacuum brake and suitable suspension, could run in passenger trains but were classified as goods wagons.

Mainline produced an OO gauge model of a Period 3 gangwayed brake van in the 1990s, which was later produced by Bachmann. There is a better model in the current Hornby range. A few years ago, Ian Allan Publishing commissioned a gangwayed 6-wheel passenger brake van from Dapol. It is a nice model but, with zero fixed wheelbase, is somewhat unstable. For wide-radius (3ft or more) curves, it benefits from having its flexible trucks fixed and better wheels. In the 1980s, Hornby produced an LMS Post Office sorting van on their generic (GWR-ish) underframe. The body was quite nice, but it was a bit short and had centre gangway connections whereas they should be offset to the loading side. It was provided with a crude working pick-up net and what looks like a tender water scoop to operate it. It was produced in LMS livery and, more recently and totally incorrectly, in Post Office Red, which was only carried by BR standard vans, and in GWR livery.

Lima produced an OO scale model of an LMS covered carrriage truck, but it has very deep wheel flanges and the wheelsets are not directly inter-changeable with Hornby, Bachmann or Jackson ones. Lima also produced a GWR horsebox in LMS livery. Hornby Dublo and Wrenn produced a 6-wheel insulated van with a nice body, but a horrible underframe. Hornby have recently introduced models of an LMS horsebox and a 4-wheel covered carriage truck.

BRITISH RAILWAYS STANDARD CARRIAGES

THE BR STANDARD MARK I CARRIAGES

After building more of each of the pre-nationaliza-tion carriage designs, British Railways produced the first of its standard carriages, now known as Mark I stock, in 1951. The carriages had all-steel bodies built on to a steel underframe fitted with buckeye couplings, giving greatly increased protection against accident damage. There were two standard underframe lengths, 57ft and 64ft. All the corri-

British Railways Mark I corridor composite S 15905 at Eastleigh 23 July 1960. It is an example of an early Mark I, built in 1955 by Metro Cammell on BR1 bogies and in crimson and cream livery.

British Railways Standard Mark I brake second M 35306 at Euston in the Up Merseyside express on 9 June 1962. It is nearly new, built to Wolverton lot number 30699, which was completed in 1963. It is mounted on Commonwealth bogies and has double-glazing and dual heating.

dor passenger carriages used the 64ft underframe. Gangwayed luggage vans were 57ft long whilst the relatively small number of non-corridor carriages were on either 57ft or 64ft frames; the LM Region used the shorter version.

A small number of BR Mark I catering vehicles and sleeping cars were built during the early 1950s, but the majority of the Mark I catering vehicles were built after 1956. Mark I carriages were initially vacuum-braked and steam-heated, but some were later built or rebuilt for electric heating and air brake.

Mark I carriages were mounted on BRI bogies, which provided a reasonable ride when new, but this deteriorated with use. Many later Mark I carriages used Commonwealth bogies with cast steel frames and equalizing beams between the axle boxes and some used LNER-designed Gresley bogies with the springs inside the frames. In later years, many Mark Is were fitted with the B4 bogies, which were introduced with the Mark 2 carriages.

BR Mark I carriages were used on all LM Region main-line express services from the 1950s, initially mixed with LMS vehicles. By about 1960, most main-line trains were formed of Mark I vehicles. There would have been some through working of carriages from main-line trains on to country branches but

the running of through carriages was much reduced by the 1960s. Mark Is were later used on relief and secondary services, but were unlikely to appear on branch lines, which were generally served by diesel multiple units.

The first OO gauge models of BR Mark I carriages were produced in the 1960s by Hornby Dublo, with printed tinplate sides on a plastic frame. They were too short, except for the BG (gangwayed brake van), which was the correct length, and still looks good in a mixed parcels train of more recent models. Tri-Ang also produced short OO gauge Mark I models in plastic, successive productions getting longer until, by the 1980s, they were approximately scale length – except for the BG, which was now too long! Mainline and Lima also produced Mark I carriages in the 1980s, of varying cross-sections and including the overlong BG.

OO gauge models of Mark I corridor carriages are currently available from both Bachmann and Hornby. Hornby produce the brake second, composite, corridor second, open second (2+1 seating), tourist open second (2+2 seating) and full brake in its Railroad range. There is a lack of fine detail, but this is not apparent when the carriages are seen in a passing train.

Mark 1 restaurant buffet (RBR) 1966 at Sheffield in the 06.57 Newcastle–Poole via Birmingham on 13 May 1989. This was built as an unclassed restaurant car (RU), which was the most numerous type of Mark 1 catering vehicle. It now has air brake and electric train supply, to work with Mark 2 carriages.

Bachmann produce a wide range of Mark 1 corridor carriages with finer detail, but at a higher price than Hornby's. These include brake composite, brake second, corridor second, tourist open second, corridor composite, corridor first, restaurant first, miniature buffet, unclassed kitchen restaurant, first and second class sleeping cars, gangwayed brake, bogie utility van and Post Office sorting van. These are available in various BR liveries, with the correct bogies for each period.

Bachmann also produce OO gauge models of the 57ft non-corridor brake second, open second and composite.

In N gauge, Graham Farish offer Mark 1 corridor and non-corridor carriages, with the same range of vehicles as the Bachmann OO gauge ones.

BR MARK 2 CARRIAGES

The British Railways Mark 2 carriage was an integrally built vehicle, with no separate underframe, running on B4 bogies and with pressure ventilation. The Mark 2s had rounded ends and wider windows than the Mark 1 design. A prototype corridor First Class carriage was built at Swindon in 1963, followed by a production batch, built at Derby in 1964, but none of these was allocated to the London Midland Region. They were the only Mark 2 vehicles to be painted in maroon or green liveries.

Full production of Mark 2 carriages started in 1966, with many of the first batch being allocated to the London Midland Region for the electrified West Coast Main Line. They all carried the corporate blue and grey livery. Compared with the Mark 1 coaches, Mark 2s were restricted to a small number of designs. All Second Class carriages were built with open-plan seating and there were no First and Second Class composites. First Class side corridor carriages were built initially, but later builds were all open-plan. There were no Mark 2 catering vehicles (although some were converted later), no sleeping

Mark 2 open second (SO) IC 5247 at Derby on 17 August 1991. This was one of the batch of coaches that went to the newly electrified West Coast Main Line in 1966 and were then vacuum-braked and dual-heated. Now, it is air-braked and has only electric heating.

Mark 2D open second (TSO) 5647 at Sheffield on 13 May 1989. It has lost its regional prefix and has InterCity lettering on its blue and grey livery. The Mark 2Cs introduced full air-conditioning with no opening windows.

cars and no full brakes. Mark 2 carriages generally ran in fixed formation sets with a Mark 1 catering vehicle between the First and Second Class and a Mark 1 gangwayed full brake at one end.

The pressure-ventilated carriages were built in batches classed Mark 2 (vacuum-braked) and 2a, 2b and 2c (air-braked). These were followed by carriages with air brake and full air conditioning, classified 2d, 2e and 2f. Pressure-ventilated Mark 2 carriages began to appear on short loco-hauled trains, replacing ageing diesel multiple units, on some of the longer cross-country services in the 1980s.

For OO gauge, Bachmann produce models of Mark 2, 2a and 2f First, Second and brake Second. They also produce the Mark 2f buffet First, which only appeared in 1988 and the driving trailer, built for Scotland. Hornby produce Mark 2d and 2e Second, First and brake Second. Graham Farish produce Mark 2a and 2f models for N gauge.

BR MARK 3 CARRIAGES

The British Railways Mark 3 carriage was a further development from the Mark 2. Although carriages were longer, computer design techniques enabled this to be achieved without significantly increased weight. The first Mark 3 carriages, built in the early 1970s, were seen as general-use vehicles, able to be hauled either by locomotives or between pairs of HST power cars. During trial operation of the

prototype HST, it became apparent that cost and weight could be saved by building carriages with 3-phase electric supply, control cables for HST power cars and no buffers for the HSTs and similar carriages, but with DC power supply, no control cables and with buffers, for locomotive haulage.

Mark 3 carriages were all built with similar body-shells, with windows to suit eight bays of First Class seating. Many seats in the Second Class did not, therefore, line up with the windows. Locomotive-hauled Mark 3s were all allocated to the London Midland Region's West Coast Main Line, where they ran in fixed formation sets with Mark 1 gang-wayed brakes at one end. Some Mark 3 catering vehicles replaced Mark 1 vehicles in the WCML's Mark 2 air-conditioned sets. A variety of catering vehicles and sleeping cars were built using the same basic bodyshell. Initially, HST sets were built with a kitchen restaurant car for First Class passengers and a buffet car for Second Class, but it was soon realized that this was an overprovision and the First Class dining cars were all transferred to the WCML.

Apart from the power supply and coupling arrangements, there is one other small difference between Mark 3 carriages built for loco haulage and HSTs. The prototype and loco-hauled carriages had two small extractor vents above each vestibule. The HST carriages have a single extractor under a square cover.

The Mark 3 carriages were all put into service on the West Coast Main Line in fixed formations, sometimes with Mark 2s in the train. A Class 87 approaching Stowe Hill tunnel on 18 September 1987 on the 13.50 Euston–Liverpool with six Mark 3 SOs, restaurant car, two FOs and a BG.

Initial allocation of HST sets was to the Western Region, followed by the East Coast Main Line. These were followed by HSTs for cross-country services via a central hub at Birmingham, which brought them on to the London Midland Region. A reorganization of allocations in the early 1980s brought HSTs on to the Midland Main Line.

Mark 3 carriages for OO gauge were built by Jouef and Hornby, followed by Lima, in the 1970s. The Jouef model was a loco-hauled Mark 3 but the others are HST vehicles. The first Hornby models were much too short, but later ones were longer, although not scale length. Currently, correct length Mark 3 versions for OO gauge are available from Hornby and due from Oxford Rail. Graham Farish and Dapol produce Mark 3s for N gauge.

PULLMAN CARS

Although the first American Pullman cars in Britain ran on the Midland Railway in the 1870s, these were later bought by the Midland and the only Pullman cars to run on the LMS were a number of dining cars from the Caledonian Railway. These were bought by the LMS and ran on Scottish internal services until the 1950s.

In 1960, the LM Region's West Coast Main Line from Euston was being badly disrupted by elec-

trification work. To provide an alternative route, services on the St Pancras–Manchester line were augmented, including the 'Midland Pullman' diesel electric Pullman car train. This was a First Class-only 6-car train that ran from Manchester to St Pancras each morning, returning to Manchester in the late afternoon, with a mid-day run from St Pancras to Leicester/Nottingham and back. At the same time, similar 8-car two-class trains were put into service on the Western Region from Paddington to Birmingham and Bristol. Once the West Coast electrification was complete, the Midland Pullmans were transferred to the Western Region and withdrawn in the early 1970s.

The Midland Pullman was produced in OO gauge kit form by Kitmaster in the 1960s, all three types of vehicle being produced. At the same time, Tri-Ang produced OO gauge models of the Western Region's Pullman motor car and a First Class trailer. These were remarkable for the time in terms of the quality of the body mouldings, with flush glazing, but were let down by being perched on Tri-Ang standard bogies. Recently, Bachmann have produced an excellent OO gauge Midland Pullman model.

On the newly electrified West Coast Main Line, the Manchester Pullman and Liverpool Pullman were put on, comprising new air-conditioned Pullman cars, based on the BR Mark 2 design. They

The Midland Pullman leaving Chinley for London St Pancras in the early 1960s. This is the Bachmann model on Famous Trains' Chinley layout.

were painted in Rail Grey with a Rail Blue band at window level. No model has been produced of the WCML Mark 2 Pullman.

DIESEL MULTIPLE UNITS

FIRST-GENERATION DIESEL MULTIPLE UNITS

The LMS tried out a few experimental diesel units in the 1930s but none survived to run on the London Midland Region. A batch of 4-wheel railbuses by British United Traction ran briefly in the early 1950s on branches from Harrow and Watford, and were followed by 2-car sets of diesel multiple units with underfloor-mounted engines and mechanical transmission. Derby Carriage Works built light-weight units, which operated on the LM and Eastern Regions, together with two single cars for the Bletchley–Banbury service. Metropolitan Cammell of Birmingham built units for the Bury–Bacup line, providing a connection with the Manchester–Bury electrics. These non-standard units were all with-drawn by 1970, but one of the single cars passed to BR Research for monitoring the signal strength of the driver-control office radio system. This is pre-served, together with a Derby 2-car unit.

Bachmann produce an OO gauge Derby light-weight model. More interesting historically, rather than in terms of its accuracy, the old Tri-Ang DMU model was based on the Bury–Bacup units, with skirting below the buffer beam.

BR MODERNISATION PLAN DIESEL MULTIPLE UNITS

Following the successful operation of the Diesel Multiple Units, large numbers were ordered from various manufacturers under the British Railways Modernisation Plan of the late 1950s. The majority of these were lightweight units, with 57ft bodies, destined for country services on the London Midland, Eastern and Scottish Regions. They were built with passenger saloons accessed from vesti-bules, with 2+3 seating on the Second Class and 2+2 seating in First Class. These ran as 2-car, 3-car and 4-car units.

There were also heavier 4-car units, with 64ft bodies, built specifically for suburban work, with multiple doors for quick loading. These were initially used by the LM Region only on London sub-urban services from St Pancras and Marylebone, with some on the Liverpool area. The Western Region opted for a mix of 3-car and single-car sub-urban units and 3-car cross-country units, with 2+2 seating in Second Class and 2+1 in First Class, all with 64ft bodies. In the 1970s, there was an exchange of units, with Western Region cross-country Class 120 units coming to the LM Region in exchange for LM Region country service units. The LM Region also acquired Western Region 3-car suburban units in the Birmingham area and by the 1980s, Tyseley depot was running mixed units of cars from different origins. The Western Region single cars became widely scattered in later years, as they were useful for inspection or driver route-learning purposes.

Some of the last first-generation DMUs were the Swindon Class 124 Trans-Pennine units and Class 123 InterCity units for the Western Region. These had higher-grade accommodation than the other units, to main-line standards, and the 123s were the only DMU cars to run on B4 bogies. In the 1970s, the 123s and 124s all passed to the Eastern Region for Trans-Pennine services, running on to the LM Region.

There were also a number of purpose-built DMU parcels cars. Cravens built two Class 129 cars for the LM Region and Gloucester RC&W Co built ten Class 128 cars, four for the LM Region without end gangways and six for the Western, with gangways. They were able to haul a tail load and moved about a bit in later years.

Most of the Diesel Multiple Units had a common control system and before long mixed formations of different builders' cars were running. During the 1970s and 1980s, there were numerous mixed formations of country service and suburban cars. A number of units were re-formed as Power Twins, giving augmented performance to stand in for delayed delivery of new units.

Numerous DMU cars are preserved on heritage railways.

A further batch of lightweight two-axle railbuses was bought from a number of builders in 1957, mainly for use in Scotland, East Anglia and the Western Region. The LM Region received some of the Park Royal cars, which ran on the Bedford–Northampton service and on the Millers Dale–Buxton line. An OO gauge model is produced by Heljan.

What is available to the modeller? Bachmann produce OO gauge models of the later Derby Lightweight Class 108 and the Cravens Class 105 units. Lima produced a Metropolitan Cammell Class 101 unit in 2- or 3-car formations, which is now produced by Hornby. Graham Farish produce N gauge models of the Metro Cammell Class 101 and the Derby Lightweight Class 108 units. Hornby used to produce an excellent OO gauge model of the Birminghan RC&W Class 110 Calder Valley units.

Derby lightweight single car M 79900 leaving Verney junction on the 18.45 Bletchley to Buckingham on 14 September 1963, as the guard collects the single line staff from the signalman. Two double-ended single railcars were built at Derby in 1957 for the Bletchley–Banbury service.

Following some early non-standard units, Metro Cammell made the largest contribution to the BR low-density fleet of diesel multiple units, with 437 cars (Class 101) built in 1956–60. A 2-car and a 3-car Metro Cammell set, with two-character headcode box, near Stanningley on a train from Leeds on 3 September 1960.

A bit of work on the window surrounds and ends could modify it to one of the more widespread Class 104 units.

Lima used to produce a Western Region Pressed Steel Class 117 suburban unit but the driving car was only available with a guard's compartment whilst the WR 3-car sets only had a guard's compartment at one end. The similar, but higher-powered, LM Region 4-car suburban sets had guard's compartments at both ends but they had an additional seating bay and smaller luggage areas. Bachmann have now announced a new OO gauge model of

the Pressed Steel Class 117 and Heljan produce one for O gauge.

The Swindon Class 120 cross-country unit is unique in being available in O gauge only, from Heljan. Trix used to produce a slightly undersized OO gauge Trans-Pennine Class 124 unit. The end cars were reasonable models but the intermediate cars were Trix Mark 1 loco-hauled carriages, and bore little resemblance to the Class 124 intermediate cars.

Lima produced an OO gauge model of the Pressed Steel Western Region Class 121 single car, which is

Birmingham Railway Carriage & Wagon Co supplied about 300 cars in 1957–58 (Class 104). MBS M 50458, TC M 59166 and MC M 50510 lead another BRC&W 3-car set at Dudley Port on the 1.15 pm Manchester–Coventry on 22 June 1963.

Derby Carriage Works built suburban units for the Western Region (Class 116) with three cars, each with two 150hp engines. Tyseley unit T321 (Class 116 DMS 53907+ Class 115 TCL 59753 + Class 115 DMBS 53854) approaching Stenson junction on the 10.18 Birmingham–Nottingham on 7 August 1991.

A 120 unit, forming the 08.52 Cambridge–Birmingham, near Wigston on 12 February 1985. The Western Region Class 120 cross-country units were built at Swindon in 1957–58 and had more spacious seating than the LM Region units. In the 1970s, there was an exchange of units between the LM and the Western.

now available from Hornby. Bachmann also produce an OO gauge Class 121 model whilst Dapol offer both a Class 121, the similar Gloucester RC&WCo Class 122, and the Pressed Steel driving trailer in both OO and N gauges. Heljan offer a Class 121 for O gauge.

Heljan produce O and OO gauge models of a Gloucester Class 128 Parcels Car.

SECOND-GENERATION DIESEL MULTIPLE UNITS

By the 1980s, the first-generation diesel multiple units were well past their initial design life. In 1982, two Class 210 diesel electric prototype units, based on the current suburban EMU design, were built. These had a single diesel engine and generator, mounted above the floor of one vehicle, and ran on the Western Region. There were no funds available to build a fleet of these trains so another approach was required.

Two-Axle Pacer Units

The British Rail Research Division had been developing two-axle freight wagon suspensions suitable

for high-speed running. In conjunction with the British Leyland Motor Corporation, a light railbus was built with a body using the components of the current Leyland National single deck bus.

Twenty Class 141 Pacer units were built at Derby with Leyland National-based bodies, to the standard bus width, in 1984. They were all allocated to West Yorkshire but were followed in 1985–86 by 100 similar Class 142 units, with wide bodies. Most of these were allocated to the LM Region and painted in the Greater Manchester PTE orange and brown livery. Pacer units of classes 143 and 144 were built with Alexander bodies but were all allocated to the Eastern or Western Regions.

An OO gauge model of a Class 142 was produced by Hornby in about 1990, with the original bus doors, and has been available until recently. RealTrack are proposing an OO gauge model, which will probably have the later doors, so will be incorrect for the LM Region period. Dapol are offering an N gauge 142, also with the later doors.

Sprinter Diesel Multiple Units

In 1984, York works built two prototype 3-car

On 15 August 1992, 142.045 in Network North West livery and 142.086 in Greater Manchester PTE livery wait at Sheffield, while 141.112 in West Yorkshire PTE livery stands on the centre road. In 1983–85, Leyland Motors and BREL built seventy 2-car 2-axle units with bodies built from Leyland National bus components. The first twenty units (Class 141) had bodies of bus width. The final fifty units (Class 142) had wider bodies.

In 1984, York Carriage Works built two prototype 3-car DMUs (Class 150.0) with 20-metre bodies similar to current suburban EMUs. These were followed by fifty 2-car units (Class 150.1) in 1985–86, which were allocated to the LM Region. 150.110 at Derby on the 11.35 to Skegness on 28 May 1988.

Class 150 diesel multiple units with 20m bodies based on the current suburban EMU design, painted in Regional Railways light grey livery with a dark blue band over the windows and a light blue waist band. After trial running in the Derby area, fifty Class 150/1 2-car units were built in 1985–86, with the light and dark blue bands transposed. Most worked on the LM Region but carried no regional M prefixes to their numbers. These were followed in 1987 by eighty-five 150/2 units with end gangways, carrying the Regional Railways livery, as used on the prototype units. Some 150/2 units were split and the cars placed in the centre of 150/1 units, which were renumbered as 150/0 3-car units.

150/1 and 150/2 units are produced for OO gauge by Bachmann and for N gauge by Graham Farish.

Super Sprinter Diesel Multiple Units

In 1987, the first of thirty-three Class 155 Super Sprinter diesel multiple units were completed at the Leyland National factory in Workington. They had 23m bodies based on Leyland National bus components and were built for long-distance cross-country services, with entry via end vestibules and end gangways. There were considerable delays in getting them into service, so they can hardly be said to have run on the LM Region. In 1991–92, all of them, except for a batch built for the West Yorkshire PTE, were rebuilt into single-car Class 153 units.

Dapol produced an OO gauge model of a Class 155 in 1990 and a single car 153 is now available from Hornby for OO gauge and from Dapol for N gauge.

Also in 1987, Metro Cammell built the first of 114 steel-bodied Class 156 2-car 23m units for long-distance cross-country services. Lima produced an OO gauge model in 1989, which is still available from Hornby. A new OO gauge 156 has been announced by RealTrack and Dapol produce one for N gauge.

ELECTRIC MULTIPLE UNITS

No survey of the rolling stock of the LM Region would be complete without a mention of electric multiple units. However, the subject is somewhat compromised in the context of this book by the complete absence of models of LM Region EMUs, apart from one model that claimed to be something else and one that only just reached the LM in the Region's final year!

A number of the lines of the LMS had been early users of electric traction for short-distance passenger services; see Chapter 9.

LMS ELECTRIC MULTIPLE UNITS

The LMS built EMUs based on its standard non-corridor carriage design for the existing London area and Southport lines, and for the Manchester–Altrincham line, which was jointly owned by the LMS and LNER. Steel-bodied saloon stock, with air-powered sliding doors, was to replace the original Southport stock and for the Wirral lines, with more

built in the 1950s to replace the Mersey Railway trains. No models are available.

LM REGION ELECTRIC MULTIPLE UNITS

The first EMUs to be delivered to the LM Region were eight 3-car units to an LNER design with sliding doors, built in 1954 for local services at the Manchester end of the 1,500V DC Manchester–Sheffield line. They were similar to units built for the Liverpool Street–Shenfield line. While the Shenfield units were rebuilt to operate on 25kV 50c/s, the Manchester units were withdrawn when the power system changed, in 1984.

In the 1950s and 1960s, British Railways built new EMUs using the Mark 1 non-corridor design, which provided the quickest unloading and loading times at stations where interchange of passengers occurred. These included new units for the LM Region's 4-rail DC London area lines, to replace the LNWR saloon stock. These were the only Mark 1 EMUs to be built on the short 57ft underframe and were initially painted in Multiple Unit Green, later replaced by Locomotive Dark Green.

When Hornby Dublo, in its last years, produced a model of an EMU, it was based on the standard Hornby non-corridor carriage, which was almost correct length for a 57ft 9-compartment vehicle. They also made the motor car with two power

LMS 1937-built Wirral line driving trailer M 29274 M leading the 10.56 Liverpool Central–West Kirby at Bidston on 5 January 1964. In 1938, the LMS built all-steel-bodied electric multiple units with sliding doors for the newly electrified Wirral lines, followed by similar but longer Metro Cammell units for the Liverpool–Southport line.

In the 1950s, Eastleigh works built 3-car units for the LM Region's London suburban services. They were similar to the Southern's 4-EPB units but with short bodies and with a single motor car on two power bogies. Hornby motor brake second 'S 65326' stands in Chinley goods yard. The number belongs to Southern 4-EPB unit 6212, but the model is clearly an LM Region London area car.

Class AM4 (later 304) 4-car units were built for the LM Region for local services on the 25kV electrified lines in the Liverpool and Manchester areas. 304.012, reduced to three cars, leaving Manchester Oxford Road on the 13.30 Alderley Edge–Altrincham on 17 December 1988.

Unit 062 at Euston in Rail Blue livery on 19 March 1966. The Mark 2-based AM 10 (later Class 310) units were built for stopping services between Euston and Birmingham.

bogies, like the LM Region London Area units, but it was only ever sold as a 'Southern Electric'.

For local services in the 25kV AC electrification area around Birmingham, Liverpool and Manchester, 4-car EMUs of class AM4 (later 304) were built to Mark I non-corridor design but with rounded ends. These were initially painted in Locomotive Dark Green. Two-car units of similar appearance (Class 504) were built to replace the LYR cars on the third rail Manchester–Bury line.

For the extension of the West Coast electrification to Euston, Class AM10 (later 310) EMUs were built, based on the Mark 2 carriage. These were gangwayed within the units, had reduced numbers of side doors and were initially painted in the Rail Blue livery.

In the 1970s, British Railways developed a family of EMUs of composite steel/aluminium construc-

tion with sliding doors. The LM Region received the third rail DC Class 507 3-car units for the Liverpool–Southport and Wirral lines in 1978. These were later joined by similar Class 508 units from the Southern, for the extension of the electrification to Chester.

In the 1980s, a family of steel-bodied EMUs was built, based on the Mark 3 carriage design. The LM Region received the first of these, the 25kV AC Class 317 4-car units for the Bedford–St Pancras electrification in 1981–82. When the Bedford–St Pancras line was joined through to the Southern in 1987/8, under the Thameslink name, the 317s were transferred to the Eastern Region and replaced by Class 319 dual-voltage units in Network South East livery.

Graham Farish produce an N gauge model of a Class 319 unit in Network South East livery.

The Class 319 dual-voltage units were built for the through service between Bedford and the Southern Region via the Metropolitan widened lines. 319.016 is at Kings Cross Thameslink on the 11.07 Bedford–Sevenoaks, on 22 May 1988, the first Sunday of through running by Thameslink trains.

An odd pair of dark green carriages, self-propelled, leaves Carlisle southbound. Each car had a Paxman 450bhp diesel engine driving a generator providing current for the motor bogie traction motors. This short-lived experiment did not go into regular passenger service. J.N. FAULKNER

The two-axle ACV diesel railbus sets gave a hard ride, but at least they worked for a few years on various LM Region branch lines. WG REAR/COLOUR-RAIL

ODD DIESEL MULTIPLE UNITS

An experimental diesel electric railcar twin unit was produced by Derby works and tested on the LM Region in 1956. Converted out of two LMS non-corridor coaches, each coach had a Paxman 450bhp diesel engine driving a generator and powering the traction motors in bogies taken from London area DC electric units. The set had a design top speed of 80mph (almost 130km/h) and was tested variously on the Midland Main Line and north to Carlisle. It quite quickly faded into oblivion, however.

No commercial models exist of it, but a modeller looking for something unusual to do might be able to modify a pair of early LMS coaches to represent the unit. Obtaining the right motor bogie type might be a challenge, though.

In addition, there were the 'flying bricks' that came from ACV. These were two-axle diesel mechanical railcars in sets, normally of three vehicles, and used on LM Region branch lines such as Watford–St Albans and Bedford–Bletchley, and also in Cumbria. They were gone by 1959. We are not aware of any commercial models of these unpopular vehicles.

Last, in the early 1980s, when British Rail was seeking some competition in design for modern DMUs to replace the first-generation DMU fleet, Metro Cammell of Birmingham delivered two Class

The Metro-Cammell answer to BR's request for a replacement for first-generation DMUs was this three-car type, designated Class 151. The prototypes remained non-standard and, after a few years in service, mainly in the Derby area, they were put into store and, much later, scrapped.

151 3-car sets to a unique design. These worked between Derby and Matlock for a while, but BR's own design, the Class 150, proved better suited to BR's needs. The Metro Cammell sets were put into store and, after many years of oblivion, were broken up.

None of these experimental diesel units has been made commercially in model form, as far as we know.

THE ADVANCED PASSENGER TRAINS

In the early 1970s, BR had a grand vision of being able to build and run trains for the West and East Coast Main Lines that could curve faster than conventional trains and would have a top speed of 150mph. Having been given free rein to innovate, engineers in BR's Research Department in Derby designed an experimental train, known as APT-E. The train had to be able travel on any main lines in the UK, including non-electrified lines. The team decided to use gas turbine electric traction. Each end car contained four small gas turbines, each driving a generator that supplied current to the traction motors. A fifth identical turbine generator set supplied electricity for train supplies and services. The middle two vehicles contained a host of electric and electronic equipment for testing and monitoring every feature of the train.

The carriages were lightweight, of aluminium construction, and the train was articulated. Each articulated bogie carried a spreader beam, the ends of which carried the adjacent carriage bodies at

The experimental advanced passenger train (APT-E) was a working test bed for a future high-speed train for British Rail. It did not enter passenger service, but is now preserved and on display at the National Railway Museum's centre at Shildon, County Durham. This OO-scale model by Rapido Trains is approaching Chinley station at the Famous Trains model railway centre.

the normal location for a 23-metre long body. This method enabled full-length carriages to be used in an articulated formation.

The carriage bodies were designed to tilt on the bogies up to 9 degrees into a curve as a way of compensating for higher speeds in those situations. The idea was that, as the train curved rapidly, the high centripetal force normally felt by passengers would be cancelled out. Because the carriage bodies were to tilt, the body profile was raked sharply inwards towards the roof, in order to maintain clearances to fixed structures when tilting.

The train was tested out of Derby, and also did some high-speed runs on the Western Region main lines. On the Midland Main Line, it created a record journey time for the London St Pancras to Leicester route, which has not been equalled since.

In 2016, Rapido Trains Inc. produced an excellent OO scale model of the APT-E train.

After evaluation, a revised set of designs was produced by BR's M&EE department. There were to be three prototype trains known as APT-P, which would go into passenger service on the West Coast Main Line. There were several significant detail design differences from APT-E, including the adoption of electric traction. The bodies were built up from longitudinal aluminium extrusions welded to form a strong but light structure. The two electric Bo-Bo power cars were located centrally in each train, because Her Majesty's Railway Inspectorate was not willing to agree to 25kV AC electric bus lines being fitted on carriage roofs along the train. (This is now common practice in the UK as it was previously in continental Europe.) The passenger units were six coaches long, fully articulated, and with a driving cab in the streamlined end vehicles. A full train therefore consisted of two sets of six passenger vehicles flanking the two power cars.

The articulation was different from that on the APT-E version because BR's designers decided to do away with the spreader beam. Instead, the coach ends were carried on air bags located on the outer end corners of each articulated bogie frame. This proved to be a major disadvantage, because the passenger ride experience in these trains was not always good. There were reports (and personal experience!) of nausea among passengers, although not on every trip. Despite these issues, the APT-P trains proved that 150mph running on the WCML was possible – although when they were put into regular passenger service, they were limited to 125mph.

A cold winter with much icing-up of brake pipes and valves, and many other faults in the detail of these trains, eventually tested BR's patience and the whole fleet was withdrawn in 1983. The tilting train idea had been proved, but the project fell down in the detail. A decade or more later, the Swedes, Italians and Japanese perfected designs of tilting trains that compensated for no more than 60 per cent of the lateral forces, and these have been in service ever since. Noteworthy in this respect are the UK's Pendolino and tilting Voyager trains, which were introduced after privatization.

Hornby did produce a very short APT-P model in a OO scale train-set pack, but never made the intermediate coaches that were articulated at both ends. Any modeller wanting to have a full-length APT-P model will need to scratch-build the intermediate coaches – it is highly unlikely that enough end coaches would ever be on the second-hand market to enable a modeller to butcher sixteen such model coaches to make up the eight needed for a full train.

During proving trials in Scotland in 1981, a full-length train of the APT-P (prototype) series traverses the Clyde Valley southbound at speed. These three trains were put into passenger service for a period of a few weeks.

CHAPTER FIVE

GOODS ROLLING STOCK

Neither the goods rolling stock that ran on British Railways London Midland Region in 1948 nor the type of goods trains that ran in the Region bore any resemblance to that which was running when the LM Region ceased to exist in 1988. The reasons for these changes are outlined in Chapter 1.

In 1948, most stations had a goods yard, generally served by a daily pick-up goods train. Most goods yards had a goods shed, an end loading dock, cattle pens and a crane. There would also be a loading gauge, to ensure that open wagons were not loaded out of gauge. Local cartage services were provided by railway-owned lorries or by contractors. If you are modelling a terminus station, you should not run any wagons that your yard facilities cannot deal with.

The main incoming traffic was coal and local coal merchants usually had offices and storage bunkers in the goods yard. Other incoming traffic, mainly in part wagon loads, included supplies for farms and local businesses, with the occasional full wagon

loads of such items as cattle or agricultural machinery. Outgoing traffic consisted of the products of the local farms, factories and other businesses. Most of this was in part wagon loads, but with some full wagon loads, particularly of cattle and seasonal agricultural produce. The local pick-up goods trains ran to marshalling yards where the wagons were shunted into main-line trains, with further shunting into another local goods train to their final destinations. Part wagon loads were generally transferred from one vehicle to another at least once before reaching their destination, often resulting in delayed or lost consignments.

Main-line goods trains generally conveyed a variety of wagons, moving from one marshalling yard to another. There were dedicated coal trains from the coal-producing areas and fast goods trains, with a proportion of vacuum-fitted wagons at the front, which conveyed mainly merchandise wagons and vans. During the 1950s and 1960s, most of this traffic was lost to road transport and the goods

English Electric 1,000hp Bo-Bo (later Class 20) D8036 approaching Kensington Olympia on a northbound goods on 11 February 1961. It is carrying the Southern's route code for a train to the LM Region via the West London line. The train includes a well wagon, with its load supported in timber beams. On the tracks behind are a number of bogie bolsters with overhanging loads, requiring the use of 2-axle flat wagons between them.

Class 8F 2-8-0 No. 48649 approaching Linslade tunnel on 27 July 1963 on a Down Class H goods. The train includes a bogie bolster wagon carrying steel girders, three open merchandise wagons, a tank wagon and a number of long-wheelbase pipe wagons. Bogie wagons carrying pre-fabricated track sections stand in the Up loop.

Class 8F 2-8-0 No. 48171 approaching Linslade tunnel on an Up Class E express goods on 27 July 1963. Vacuum-braked vans form the visible part of the train; the first three vans are LMS, BR and LNER and there are some Southern elliptical roofs visible through the smoke. Overhead structures for the coming electrification are beginning to appear.

RIGHT: A WD 2-8-0 approaching Bowling tunnel on a goods train for Bradford Exchange goods depot on 3 September 1960. The train consists mainly of vans, but there is one sheeted open wagon and a container wagon towards the rear of the train.

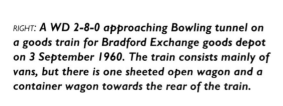

Derby/Sulzer 1,250hp Type 2 Bo-Bo 25279 at Spondon, ready to return to Derby on an air-braked trip working from the British Celanese plastics factory on 7 July 1986. At the front of the train are three VCA vans, with two quarter-length doors each side, two in brown and one in red/grey. These are followed by a tank wagon, which might well be continental, then an open and more vans.

yards were closed, to be sold off or to become station car parks. Many factories had their own private railway sidings, but most of these were also removed during the 1960s.

The British Railways Modernisation Plan of the 1950s sought to reduce costs by introducing more automated marshalling yards but retaining many of the old freight train-operating practices. With the coming of air-braked wagons, in the 1970s, 'Speedlink' freight services were introduced for wagon-load traffic but never developed any great amount of business. British Railways began to concentrate on the operation of train loads of bulk material, such as coal, aggregates and oil, with 'Freightliner' container trains to carry general goods, in particular to and from seaports.

BRITISH RAILWAYS GOODS ROLLING STOCK

British Railways inherited about one and a quarter million wagons in 1948. These were almost all small 4-wheeled wagons with only hand lever brakes. There had been moves by a number of the old railway companies to introduce larger bogie wagons in the early years of the twentieth century, but they were resisted by the customers, who did not want the cost of adapting their premises to deal

with these larger wagons. There were also about 200,000 privately owned wagons on the system, mostly owned by oil companies and other mineral producers. Most types of wagon were 'common user', so there is no need to restrict wagons on an LM Region layout to ex-LMS or BR standard types.

The livery adopted for British Railways wagons in 1948 was light grey for those only fitted with handbrakes, and bauxite, a reddish-brown, for those fitted with vacuum brake. Underframes were generally black for steel-framed wagons or body

Two LMS 13T open merchandise wagons on timber underframes at Eastleigh, Southern Region, on 29 July 1960. These are general-purpose wagons, which might be loaded with anything apart from minerals, and were covered by a tarpaulin sheet if the load required protection from the weather.

colour for timber-framed wagons, but there were exceptions. Old companies' wagons retained their old numbers, with E, M, S or W prefixes indicating their origin. British Railways standard wagons had a B prefix and ex-private owner wagons a P prefix. Unlike carriages, there was no specific allocation of wagons to the Regions. The number and load were in white characters on a black panel at the bottom left of the side of grey wagons and painted directly on the brown wagons, with the tare weight at bottom right. Departmental wagons were generally black with a DM, DB, and so on, prefix. Flat wagons had the number painted on the frames, which were generally body colour. In the 1970s, the number panels received white edges.

When the British Rail's Railfreight subsidiary was set up in the 1980s, wagons were painted light grey with a Flame Red top band for traffic wagons and a yellow band for departmental wagons.

COAL WAGONS

Although the railway companies provided some wagons for the transport of coal, until 1948 the majority of this traffic was carried in wagons owned by the mineral producers or users. There were about 500,000 coal wagons, most built to the 1923 Railway Clearing House (RCH) specification, owned by collieries, coal factors and coal merchants. Wagon utilization was low, with wagons being used for storage and being returned when empty to defined collieries. In 1939, all these wagons were requisitioned by the Government and placed in a general pool, which passed to British Railways in 1948. Some were repainted but many retained the remains of their old owners' liveries, with P prefix numbers. They were almost entirely wooden wagons of 10–13T capacity on 9ft wheelbase timber underframes, although some were on steel frames. Some had side doors only, while others also had end and bottom doors.

Bachmann, Dapol and Oxford Rail all produce OO gauge models of RCH coal wagons in a variety of liveries, including BR grey. Numerous models were produced by Mainline and Airfix in the 1980s,

but these were based on a standard 10T steel underframe, so they look too long when mixed with more recent models. Hornby produce a smaller 10T wagon with a variety of bodies, but few of these would have been running by 1950. Graham Farish produce RCH coal wagon models for N gauge and Dapol for O gauge. Many easily built plastic kits are available for OO and O gauge, enabling the appearance of a greater variety of wagons.

There were small numbers of larger all-steel wagons, including some built by the railway companies and by the Ministry of War Transport. Between 1949 and 1963, the wooden wagons were replaced by about 240,000 steel 16T wagons. These had end and side doors, and the early ones had bottom doors as well. Some of the later ones were fitted with vacuum brake. There were about 10,000 larger wagons of 21–24T capacity, but these were mainly used in South Wales and the North East, where about 30,000 hopper coal wagons were also in use.

Bachmann produce models of a variety of 16T steel mineral wagons for OO gauge, to which Parkside-Dundas kits, recently taken into the Peco range, enable more varieties to be added. The old Airfix plastic kit from the 1950s is still produced by

Two Diagram 108 16T mineral wagons in a northbound goods at Midford on the Somerset & Dorset on 31 August 1965, when the Somerset coalfield was still working. Diag 108, the most common of the BR 16T mineral wagons, had side and end doors only, and was fitted with Morton brakes.

IMPROVING THE AIRFIX/DAPOL 16T MINERAL WAGON KIT

Over the past fifty years, many modellers will have built the Airfix 16T Mineral Wagon kit, now still in production by Dapol. It represents a wagon to Diagram 106 (see next page) with side, end and bottom doors, 1,500 of which were built in 1949, with independent brake gear on either side. Subsequently, over 200,000 wagons to Diagram 108 (see previous page) were built without bottom doors and with Morton brake gear, in which the brakes are linked by a cross shaft and one brake lever operates through a dog clutch, reversing the movement of the cross shaft. Most wagons had the brakes on the non-clutch side removed.

In an odd quirk on the brake gear of the Airfix/Dapol kit (see below, left), if you push the brake lever down, the cross shaft rotates clockwise and the brakes move away from the wheels! One simple way of rectifying this problem is to reverse the brake mouldings (see bottom left).

Before fixing the brake levers to the wagon, its appearance may be further enhanced by the removal of the odd triangular fillet from the V-hanger. The overscale door hinges may also be removed; they are not needed unless you wish to have an opening door. The downside is that the fine detail on the brake gear is now on the back. The V on the side door indicates the presence of a bottom door.

In a further alteration, the brake lever has been cut off the V-hanger and reattached above a plasticard boss, to represent the reversing dog clutch of the Morton brake gear on a Diagram 108 wagon. A cross shaft of plastic rod has been added and the only brake gear on the other side is the brake lever and V-hanger. The brakes and Morton clutch were generally on the side of the wagon with the end door to the left.

Note that all these wagons have had finer tension link couplings fitted, to leave only enough gap between the buffers for curves of 3ft radius. This improves the appearance of a train of wagons.

Airfix/Dapol Diag 106 16T mineral wagon, as built from the kit, without alterations.

Airfix/Dapol Diag 106 16T mineral wagon with modified single side brake gear.

Airfix/Dapol Diag 108 16T mineral wagon with Morton brake gear.

A Diagram 106 16T mineral wagon at Gloucester in a westbound empty coal train on 23 March 1963. This wagon has side, end and bottom doors, indicated by the white diagonal stripe and the V on the side door, and has two independent sets of brakes.

Dapol and makes a nice low-cost wagon, but it is fitted with a curious arrangement of brake gear, in which the brake comes off when the hand lever is pushed down! This fault is easily corrected during assembly by reversing the brake rigging. Graham Farish produce a 16T mineral wagon for N gauge and Dapol for O gauge. Peco also produce an N gauge model, but it is too long.

From the mid-1960s, the 16T mineral wagon, which spent most of its time as a static coal store, was replaced by the 'merry-go-round' HAA wagon, which, in theory, never stopped moving, being loaded and unloaded on the move. This one is seen arriving at Willington Power Station on 21 June 1995, so post-dates the LM Region but, apart from the blue Mainline panel, it would have been the same ten or twenty years earlier.

58014, in Railfreight Grey with coal sector markings, passing Stenson Junction on a train of empty HAA 'merry-go-round' coal wagons on 27 August 1991.

'Merry-go-round' train entering Chinley station on the Famous Trains model railway. The loco is a Hornby Class 56 and the wagons are weathered Hornby Railroad.

In the late 1960s, British Railways introduced the concept of 'merry-go-round' coal movement between collieries and power stations. Under this system, fixed formations of air-braked wagons were run from loading points at the collieries to unloading points at the power stations. With all the collieries owned by the National Coal Board and the power stations by the Central Electricity Generating Board, British Railways were able to demonstrate that investment in new loading and unloading plant would enable all three bodies to benefit from cost savings, compared with the old methods of individual wagon operation. Between 1966 and 1982, about 9,000 35½T capacity air-braked HAA hopper wagons were built for this traffic.

These wagons would have run only in block loads between collieries and power stations. At the same time, 2,000 HEA hoppers, without provision for automatic unloading, were built for other coal traffic. A number of coal concentration depots were built, from which the coal was delivered to individual consumers by road.

Hornby produce an HAA wagon for OO gauge and both Hornby and Bachmann produce an HEA. Graham Farish produce an N gauge HAA and Dapol produce both HAA and HEA wagons for O gauge.

OIL TANK WAGONS

During the 1948–70 period, all commercial movement of oil on British Railways was in wagons owned by the oil companies. In 1948, these were mostly unbraked two-axle wagons of about 14–20T capacity. Class A tanks, carrying the more inflammable oils, were painted silver and Class B tanks, for the less inflammable oils, were black. During the Second World War all the tank wagons had been pooled and Class A tanks painted grey, but the individual company identities, on silver or grey Class A tank and black Class B tanks, returned from about 1950. There were numerous oil distribution depots at, or close to, the major towns, to which oil tanks were brought in small numbers in mixed goods trains.

9F 2-10-0 92231 approaching Winchester, on the ex-GWR Didcot–Southampton line, on a block oil train from Fawley refinery to Bromford Bridge on 4 March 1961. It is not on the LM Region but it is going there! Behind the two barrier wagons are a string of unbraked Esso tank wagons of considerable variety and age.

92231 again, on the same train but further north, approaching Burghclere summit on 26 June 1962. The train now consists entirely of vacuum-braked 35T tank wagons. The 35T vacuum-braked tanks had a fairly short life as, by the 1970s, air-braked 100T bogie tanks were usual.

Hornby and Bachmann both produce 14T cradle-mounted tank wagons for OO gauge, based on the Mainline model from the 1970s and Hornby also produce the 20T tank, first made by Airfix. Bachmann also produce an anchor-mounted tank wagon for OO gauge. For N gauge, tank wagons are produced by Graham Farish and Peco and Dapol produce a 1939 Air Ministry tank wagon for O gauge. Many of these models are produced in a variety of colourful liveries of doubtful authenticity.

During the 1950s, the local rail-served oil depots were superseded by a smaller number of large distribution centres, served by block trains. Vacuum-braked 35T gross weight wagons began to appear, followed by 50T wagons in the 1960s. 100T gross weight air-braked bogie tanks first appeared in 1966. During the 1970s, tank wagon ownership passed mainly to leasing companies and the oil company logos disappeared – along with any attempts at keeping the outside of the wagons clean.

There were still a number of workings of oil tanks to individual consumers and to British Railways' own locomotive depots.

As soon as Esso put its first vacuum-braked 35T gross weight tank wagons into service in the late 1950s, Airfix produced an OO gauge plastic kit, which is still available from Dapol. Oxford Rail have announced OO gauge models of both Class A (light oil, grey) and Class B (heavy oil, black) tanks. Heljan produce both OO and O gauge models.

Moving into the air-brake period, the 45T TTA tank wagon is produced by Bachmann and Hornby for OO gauge and Graham Farish and Peco for N gauge. The TEA 100T bogie tank wagon is produced by Bachmann, Hornby and Revolution/Rapido for OO gauge and by Graham Farish and Revolution Trains in N gauge.

OTHER MINERAL WAGONS

Specific wagons were built for transporting bulk minerals such as crushed stone, iron ore, sand or china clay. Some were railway-owned, while others belonged to the mineral producers. Most moved in wagonloads but there were some block trains in the 1950s, mainly local to the mineral-producing areas. The numbers of block trains, and distances run, increased from the 1970s.

Stone and iron ore were much heavier than coal, so the wagons were generally smaller than coal wagons for a given load. They were often hoppers or doorless tippler wagons, emptied in a rotating frame. Stone or ore were sometimes carried in part-loaded coal wagons.

For OO gauge, Hornby and Bachmann produce tippler wagons; Bachmann and Dapol produce hopper wagons. For N gauge, Graham Farish produce tipplers and hoppers. Hattons have announced an OO gauge model of the ICI bogie limestone wagons, which ran between Tunstead Quarry (Buxton) and their Northwich chemical works from 1936 to 1994. As the FTMR layout represents Chinley station, we already have two sets of sixteen wagons, scratch-built from plasticard at a fraction of the price, but without the fine detail that the Hattons model will offer.

GENERAL MERCHANDISE WAGONS

After mineral wagons, general-purpose merchandise wagons were the most numerous type in British Railways' fleet. The following table lists the number of merchandise wagons owned at the start of years 1948, 1958 and 1968. It shows clearly the decline in goods transport by rail during the 1960s and the increased use of vans, in place of open wagons.

A train of twenty-six empty PHV vacuum-braked ex-ICI limestone hoppers arriving at Peak Forest behind 37407 and 37509 on 6 September 1996, near the end of their sixty-year service life. The overall dark brown weathered 'livery' of the exterior of the wagons contrasts with the interior, which has been scoured white by the limestone.

A loaded limestone train passing through Chinley on the Famous Trains layout. The loco is the powerful Hornby Dublo 8F and the wagons are all scratch-built.

Year	Open wagons	Covered vans	Total	% vans
1948	324,000	147,000	471,000	31.2
1958	302,000	150,000	452,000	33.0
1968	74,000	69,000	143,000	48.4

(*British Goods Wagons* by R.J. Essery, D.P. Rowland and W.O. Steel, David & Charles 1970)

Much general goods traffic was conveyed in open wagons, with a tarpaulin sheet to protect the load if required. Merchandise wagons differed from mineral wagons in having wider side doors, the full height of the bodyside, with low, medium and high sides. All four of the pre-1948 companies had built large numbers of merchandise wagons, of about 12T capacity, which were common user and could turn up anywhere in Britain. The largest companies, the LMS and the LNER, had built all-timber merchandise wagons until about 1930, then wagons with timber bodies on steel underframes, some of which were fitted with vacuum brakes. The final LNER design, with a steel body, was then built by British Railways until 1957, together with further timber-bodied wagons. The BR wagons, and some of the old companies' wagons, were vacuum-braked and some had sheet rails for tarpaulins. One variety was the shock wagon, with a shorter body fitted with longitudinal springs to enable it to move on its underframe, to reduce shunting shocks to fragile loads.

Bachmann produce an LNER/BR steel-bodied merchandise wagon and a timber-bodied shock wagon for OO gauge and Oxford Rail produce an LNER merchandise wagon. Graham Farish produce both steel- and timber-bodied merchandise wagons for N gauge and Dapol for O gauge.

In the 1970s, air-braked long-wheelbase merchandise wagons were built for the short-lived 'Speedlink' freight services. For OO gauge, Bachmann produce models of the timber-bodied OBA and steel-bodied

A refined version of the open goods was the shock wagon, with the body built to slide on the frame, with longitudinal springs to absorb shocks received during shunting. Four shock wagons are being loaded with slates at Minffordd, on the former Cambrian Railways, on 10 July 1964. The southbound Class H goods behind Class 3 2-6-2T 82034 has only two vans, but might pick up more on its trundle down the coast.

OCA wagons, whilst Graham Farish produce OAA, OBA and OCA wagons for N gauge and Heljan produce an OAA for O gauge.

COVERED GOODS VANS

Covered goods vans, like merchandise wagons, had been built by all the old companies and were common user. The LNER continued to use timber underframes through the 1920s, but all the others had timber bodies of about 12T capacity on steel underframes, and some later LMS vans had pressed steel corrugated ends. During the Second World War, the Southern had built its distinctive elliptical-roofed vans for the GWR and LMS. Some vans from all the companies were vacuum-braked.

The British Railways covered goods van was a development of the GWR design, with the LMS corrugated steel ends, and vacuum brake. There was also a shockvan version and vans with wide doors, to carry palletized loads. All the companies had built versions of their covered vans for specialized transport of perishable goods such as fruit, meat and fish.

For OO gauge, Bachmann produce models of all the old companies' covered goods vans and the BR standard van, together with an LNER fish van, GWR motor car van and shockvan and a BR insulated van. Both Hornby and Dapol produce models of the BR fish van and Dapol produce a GWR long-wheelbase

fruit van. For N gauge, Graham Farish produce models of the LNER, Southern and BR covered goods vans and Dapol produce the BR fish van and GWR long-wheelbase fruit van. Dapol produce a model of the BR van for O gauge.

In the 1970s, British Railways built a range of air-braked long-wheelbase covered vans and some 12T vans were rebuilt with new suspension and air brakes. Commercial traffic failed to develop but some were used for Ministry of Defence traffic into the 1990s. For OO gauge, Bachmann produce

An LMS banana van at Southampton on 15 August 1962. It is double-skinned and fitted with steam heating as well as vacuum brakes. At that time, it was usual to carry bananas in refrigerated ships, but to start the ripening process during the onward rail journey, in block trains of steam-heated vans.

The successors of the 12T van were a series of air-braked long-wheelbase vans built in the 1970s. This is a VAA, with sliding doors, half the length of the van, at Didcot on 28 July 1991. It is in the Railfreight Red and Grey livery, introduced in the 1980s.

models of the short-wheelbase VEA van and the long-wheelbase VAA, VDA, VGA and VIX (ferry) vans. Graham Farish produce the VBA and VGA vans for N gauge and Heljan produce a VAA van for O gauge.

CONTAINER WAGONS

The origins of container traffic by rail go back to the nineteenth century, with containers being used by household removal contractors and for other specialized operations. More general use of containers developed in the 1930s, led by the LMS. Initially, any suitable flat wagons or low-sided open wagons were used to carry the containers, but specialized container wagons with chain pockets were developed and, by about 1960, only these specialized wagons were allowed to be used for container traffic. A range of containers in 8ft (Type A) and 16ft (Type B) lengths were built.

For OO gauge, Bachmann, Hornby and Dapol all produce BR Conflat wagons, with container loads, and Bachmann produce a 3-plank wagon with a container load. Graham Farish and Peco produce Conflat models for N gauge.

British Railways introduced the Liner Train

A pair of FGAs at Totton Hants. In the 1960s, British Railways saw container transport as the future for most of its non-bulk freight. Between 1964 and 1976, 850 'outer' FGA container wagons, with buffers at one end, and 1275 'inner' FFA wagons were built at Shildon and Ashford. Today, a wide variety of container wagons run in trains of various types of wagon but, during the LM Region period, the FGA and FFA wagons, generally in sets of five, were the only ones to be seen.

A Class 47, in blue livery with small double arrows, passing St Cross, Winchester, on a Freightliner from the north to Southampton Docks on 7 June 1986.

Hornby FFA with the body lowered and buffer beams added to make a FGA.

concept of air-braked container trains in 1965, coinciding with the development of international maritime container transport. It later passed to British Rail's Freightliner subsidiary. The initial wagons were formed into fixed rakes of three low-floor FFA wagons between two FGAs, with buffers at the outer ends. These were the only Freightliner wagons in use during the LM Region period.

Hornby produced a crude model of an FFA in 1969, which is still available in its Railroad range. It is too high mounted and there is no FGA to run with it. Bachmann have recently announced FFA and FGA models.

LIVESTOCK VANS

Since the nineteenth century, livestock vans had been distinctively different from other covered vans. They were generally somewhat longer, the upper part of the sides was open and doors were in three pieces, the bottom flap dropping down on to the loading dock to enable the livestock to walk in or out. All four of the old companies had built vans of this type. Bodies were timber, as were the underframes of earlier LMS and LNER vans. Most were vacuum-braked or piped and all were common user. British Railways cattle vans were based on the GWR design and the last were built in 1954. Cattle traffic was not subject to common carrier regulations and British Railways stopped carrying livestock after the 1950s, apart from some recognized heavy flows of cattle, which had finished by the 1970s.

For OO gauge, the only model of an LMS cattle van is Bachmann's version of the Mainline model from the 1980s, which is too short. Bachmann produce a model of a GWR and BR standard cattle van, Hornby do a Southern van and Oxford Rail an LNER van. Graham Farish produce the GWR and BR vans for N gauge.

SPECIALIZED WAGONS

Wagons were also built for specific traffics such as bulk powders, steel, and other indivisible heavy loads.

Bulk powders such as salt and lime were generally carried in private owner wagons, similar to coal wagons, but with a pitched roof to protect the load. Unlike coal wagons, these continued to be privately owned in the early British Railways period. Bachmann, Dapol and Hornby all produce OO gauge models in a variety of colourful private owner liveries, while Peco produce N gauge models.

In the 1950s, bulk powder wagons, unloaded by air pressure, were introduced. For OO gauge, Airfix produced plastic kits in the 1950s for Presflo and Prestwin wagons, which are still available from Dapol. Bachmann produce ready-to-run OO gauge models of these wagons and Graham Farish produce a Presflo for N gauge. Hornby produce an OO gauge model of the PCA bulk powder tank from the 1970s.

Unpressurized covered hopper wagons were built for grain traffic and other powders. Bachmann and Dapol produce OO gauge models of grain hoppers and Bachmann produce a Covhop, used for other powder traffic. For N gauge, Dapol produce a grain van and Graham Farish a Covhop.

STEEL-CARRYING WAGONS

Specialized wagons were built to carry steel plates and tubes and for part-processed steel. In the early LM Region days, these would generally have been moved by mixed goods trains, but specific steel trains became usual in later days. In OO gauge, Bachmann produce models of BR tube wagons, pipe wagons and plate wagons for the earlier period and an SPA plate wagon and BAA bogie coil wagon for the air-brake period. For N gauge, Peco produce plate and tube wagons and Graham Farish a pipe wagon and an air-braked BAA coil wagon.

CAR-CARRYING WAGONS

From the start of main-line railways, wagons have been provided for carrying road carriages, and these continued into the age of the motor car. Motorail trains, conveying passengers in ordinary carriages and their cars in separate wagons, were popular from the 1960s to the 1980s. Transport of new cars in block trains became common in the 1960s, using underframes from redundant passenger carriages and specialized car-carrying vehicles have since been built. For OO gauge, Bachmann produce a Lowfit, for carrying a single vehicle, and have announced a Carflat on a BR Mark I underframe, while Oxford Rail produce a car carrier on an LMS carriage underframe. The N Gauge Society produce a BR Mark I-based carflat for its own members. The Hornby Railroad range includes a basic model of a double-deck Motorail car transporter and Bachmann produce an IPA twin car transporter from the late 1970s.

HEAVY OR LONG LOAD WAGONS

Specialized wagons for carrying heavy or long loads have been around since the nineteenth century. The most common vehicles were the two-axle or bogie machinery wagon, with dropped or load-carrying area, and the bolster wagon, a short flat wagon with a transverse swivelling bolster, two of which could carry a long load, and the longer double bolster or bogie bolster wagon.

In OO gauge, Hornby produce a model of an LNER or BR Lowmac two-axle machinery truck and Bachmann produce an LNER or BR Weltrol bogie

well wagon. Oxford Rail and Hattons have both announced models of Warwell bogie well wagons, built during the Second World War for transporting tanks, and Bachmann have announced the associated Warflat, without the dropped centre. Hattons have announced a Warwell for O gauge. Both these wagon types were later used on British Railways. For OO gauge, an LNER, LMS or BR two-axle double bolster wagon has been announced by TMC/Bachmann, while a GWR bogie bolster wagon is produced by Hornby and a BR Bogie Bolster C and an air-braked BDA bogie bolster are produced by Bachmann. For N gauge, Peco offer pairs of single bolster wagons and a two-axle twin bolster wagon, while Graham Farish offer a Bogie Bolster C and an air-braked BDA wagon, and DJ Models a Bogie Bolster E.

BRAKE VANS

Until the 1970s, all goods trains conveyed a brake van at the tail of the train. This provided accommodation for the guard and was essential while wagons fitted only with hand-operated brakes were in use. With the elimination of hand-braked wagons and the introduction of diesel locomotives, it became possible to eliminate the brake van from goods trains fitted with automatic brakes throughout. The

The railways had numerous special wagons to carry unusual or large loads. This is Swindon on 25 June 1966, where concrete bridge girders are being carried on wagon B 901150, which is described as a 45ft 50T Weltrol to Diagram 2/738. Its two ends have been separated, with two container wagons and a long-wheelbase flat wagon in between.

guard was then accommodated in the rear cab of the locomotive. Brake vans remained in use into the 1980s, particularly on engineers' trains.

Each of the old companies had its own design of brake van and these generally remained on their originating Regions during the British Railways period, although some wandering occurred. LMS, LNER and Southern brake vans had a central cabin with guard's side lookouts, containing the hand-brake and vacuum brake, where fitted. There were access platforms at either end, with open platform extensions on Southern and later LNER vans. The Southern also had some bogie brake vans for use on express goods trains, some of which were fitted with air brake and used on departmental services on the LM Region in the 1980s. GWR vans had no side lookouts and only one end balcony, which con-tained the handbrake. These vans would not have been welcome off the Western Region. The first LMS brake van was based on a Midland Railway design and was superseded by a longer design during the 1930s. The British Railways standard van was derived from the final LNER design.

For OO gauge, Bachmann produce models of the late Midland and early LMS vans, while Hornby produce the later LMS van. Both Hornby and Bachmann produce models of the LNER and BR standard brake van, while Bachmann produce both two-axle and bogie Southern brake vans. For N gauge, Graham Farish produce models of both types of LMS and the BR standard brake van. The only ready-to-run O gauge brake van is the Dapol Southern two-axle van, somewhat similar to the LNER/BR van. Some of these ran on LM Region engineers' trains in the 1980s.

DEPARTMENTAL WAGONS

Ballast wagons have been built in a variety of forms, from dropside wagons to side tippers and hoppers, in both two-axle and bogie variants. British Railways gave all its ballast wagons 'Fishcode' titles, although many of the names were not fish. For OO gauge, Dapol produce the Grampus dropside wagon, Flangeway the Mermaid side tipper, Bachmann the Sealion bogie hopper, and Hornby the Turbot two-axle hopper and the Shark plough brake van. For N gauge, DJ Models produce the Shark and Mermaid, Graham Farish the Sealion and Dapol the Grampus.

An LMS 20T brake van at Swindon on 23 March 1963. This was the final design of LMS van, built into the early British Railways period. This one is vacuum-braked but others were provided with hand brakes only. The purpose of the brake van was to assist the engine driver to control trains of unbraked wagons; all goods trains had to have a brake van at the rear. During the 1970s, this requirement was dropped for trains with automatic brakes throughout, and the guard rode in the rear cab of the locomotive.

CHAPTER SIX

STRUCTURE MODELLING

MODELLING REAL PLACES

If the place you choose to model still exists, then a camera, tape measure and possibly a helper are all you need to get started. If you can include your helper, or a measuring stick of known height in your pictures, then working out the dimensions of a building is straightforward.

Once the dimensions are known, each aspect of the building may be marked out on paper, using the scale appropriate to the model. The scales are common: 4mm = 1 foot for OO scale, 7mm = 1ft for O scale and 2mm = 1ft for N scale.

If you are modelling a building that is no longer there, or which has been heavily modified, you may well be able to go to the archives and find scale drawings of what you want. The internet is an excellent source for old pictures and plans.

Sometimes you have to work from old photographs, which may not show you every view. These may be difficult to scale, but if you work from the common size of a modern door being 6ft 6 inches in height (28mm in OO scale), it will be possible to calculate dimensions. If the building dates from earlier times, you should take into consideration the fact that doors were rarely more than 6ft in height (24mm).

If you are making a freelance model, it is still worth basing your buildings on real examples. Look at pictures of real stations in the approximate area in which you want to set your model. What features do they have in common? Look at the type of roof, style of windows and doors, chimneys, general layout, type of construction material used and colours of paintwork.

If you work from these ideas, your model will be recognizable as correct. Whatever structures you are including – stations, signal boxes, goods sheds, lineside sheds, fencing, signals, overhead wires and buildings along the route – you will need to base your models on real examples.

STRUCTURE MODELLING

Whatever structure you are planning to build, whether it is a lineside shed, a house, a station or a viaduct, the most important thing to bear in mind is ensuring that the model has internal strength.

MODELLING STONE

Many parts of the London Midland Region travel through areas where stone was a major part of building construction. There are a number of ways to approach structures built from stone, including embossed plastic sheet, which will achieve quite quick results. However, it is not a good idea to make the whole structure from embossed sheet. Use the textured sheet to cover a sound base, made from thicker plastic sheet, mounting board (2mm thick card), foamboard or even thin MDF. Foamboard is a sandwich of dense plastic foam between two sheets of thin card. This will give the model strength to withstand damp or wide variations in temperature, which often affect those who model in sheds or lofts. Colour the plastic with enamel or acrylic paints, but be careful to use matt paints as a shiny finish spoils the effect.

Another easy way to model stonework, especially if the stones are regular in shape and laid in courses, is to cover the basic structure with strips of cartridge paper, to show the courses. Use a sharp miniature screwdriver to emboss the vertical joints along each strip. This is a task that can take a long time, but the results are well worth the effort.

Where you want to model random stone effects on buildings, it is best to work on a really solid structure – possibly 2mm MDF, or 5mm thick foamboard – with plenty of internal support. This

The Prince's Hotel on the Famous Trains layout is of card construction with an overlay of Wills plastic sheet. Paper quoins on the corners cover the otherwise visible ends of the plastic. The model is painted in acrylic paint. C. NEVARD, MODEL RAIL

A model of the exchange shed on the Cromford canal, made for the Famous Trains layout. It is built from 5mm thick foamboard and the regular stone courses are represented by horizontal strips of cartridge paper, with the vertical joints embossed with a sharpened jeweller's screwdriver. It is painted in a mixture of acrylic paint and watercolour.

TOP LEFT: *The shell of a structure made from 5mm thick foamboard, showing internal strengtheners to stop warping.*

MIDDLE LEFT: *Following a thin layer of PVA glue, the 'polyfilla' layer is added to about 1mm thickness.*

BELOW: *When dry, the polyfilla is scribed with stones and given a light wash of paint, to highlight the scoring.*

Doors and windows are then added and finally a roof is fitted, using card covered with strips of cartridge paper, cut to show slates, and painted.

A completed filler-covered model, based on a Petite Properties kit, made from MDF. Downpipes have been added and the roof completed with a downloaded printed tie sheet, cut into strips and fixed with PVA glue.

is because the structure will be covered first by a thin cover of PVA glue and then by a final thin layer of quick-drying 'polyfilla'. A structure that is not well supported internally is likely to bend and twist as the plaster coat dries, leading to it flaking off. Some modellers prefer to use a thin layer of air-drying clay such as Das.

Once the covering of filler has dried, it can be lightly sanded smooth, to achieve an even finish, and then the shape of each stone may be carved gently into the surface. An old compass or a scribing tool will work well, but any sharp pointed tool can be used. Once the model has been scribed, it may be painted with a thin wash of paint, to highlight the grooves between the stones, and then the individual stones can be painted separately.

The big advantage of using filler is its absorbency, which allows the use of watercolour paint. This type of paint dries quickly and is easily blended.

There are some excellent proprietary base models available, which are easy to use to make convincing stone models. Many are now laser-cut and very strong.

MODELLING IN BRICK

Much of the London Midland Region in cities and towns has structures built of the local brick. As well as ready-to-build models in card and plastic, which

Cottages built from card that has been scribed directly with brick courses and painted with watercolours.

A close-up of some embossed card brick paper, which has been coloured with pencil crayons and weathered with weathering powders.

cover almost any building you might wish to make, there are also excellent downloadable models available, and, more recently, some very detailed ready-made models in resin from Bachmann and Hornby, which show details beautifully.

Should you wish to model a specific builing, there are a number of materials available to represent textured brickwork, from Wills or Slater's plastic sheets and embossed card from Howard Scenics to smooth brick paper from many manufacturers, including excellent downloadable sheets. If you have the time and patience, a scribing tool or an old pair of compasses may be used to scribe horizontal grooves on plain card walls, to represent the courses, and then the verticals may be added using a sharpened jeweller's screwdriver. Make sure the pattern of bricks, known as the bond, is correct for the building being modelled.

Again, you need to ensure that the structure has a sound basic form before adding the brickwork. Embossed card brickwork may be coloured with watercolour paints or even with coloured pencil crayons. If you choose this method, colour with the edge of the point diagonally across the bricks to avoid colouring too heavily between the joints. Colour plastic brickwork with either enamel or acrylic paints, again aiming for a matt surface finish. There are many publications that describe how to do this with a number of excellent alternative methods that are relevant for any Region being modelled.

ROOFS AND CHIMNEYS

Roofs and chimneys are the most visible part of any model, so care is needed to make these look right. Embossed plastic is the simplest way to add roofing,

Three different types of roof finish – roofs are the most visible part of any railway model. In the foreground is a ready-printed slate roof on a card kit. On the row of buildings to the rear, two roofs are finished with Wills plastic slates and one is finished with rows of individually applied slates.

but using strips of notched card to represent tiles or slates, or even adding separate slates cut from paper, can create the most realistic of roofs. This is especially relevant when the model is of an old building with a sagging roofline.

ROWS OF HOUSES

If you are modelling a city or town layout, one really necessary feature will be the rows of terraced house backs that run alongside the tracks approaching the station. There are very many models of such buildings, in both full and low relief. These include card structures by Metcalfe or Superquick, for example, or plastic or ready-made resin models by Hornby or Bachmann. Others are available to download, print and assemble.

At first glance, these terraces are all alike, but each house is its own variation on the theme. The backyards and in particular gardens are perfect for adding interesting details, especially at the railway end, where they often become untidy and overgrown. As most of these structures were built after the railway arrived, they are likely to be made of brick rather than stone and will be very grimy with smoke and dirt from the railway itself. Even on a later-era model, the grime is unlikely to have gone!

Allotments were also very often fitted into the spaces left between railway infrastructure and houses. These were very prominent around both towns and villages in the London Midland Region area and are always an interesting feature to model.

INDUSTRIAL FEATURES

Many parts of the London Midland Region were important for industry, in particular heavy industry. Coal mining, in particular, was a predominant feature across the Midlands and into the North West.

Advice on how to model a complete coal mine would be beyond the remit of this book, but a representation of a mine, in a corner of a layout, together with some of the sidings associated with it, will make a really interesting feature. It also provides an excuse for a lot of coal traffic. Both Hornby and

A mill or factory complex assembled from Metcalfe Kits. Most have been adapted in some way and all have been weathered with weathering powders.

The Ratio two-bay signal box, the windows from which were used to improve the Dapol kit. (The windows are available separately.) It is built straight out of the box, with no modifications. By the 1950s the real box had no railings. It is similar to the Churchward model and is shown here at Chinley station at Famous Trains. Note the Midland-style fencing.

Bachmann make superb resin models of the kind of buildings you might find at a colliery, including the pithead gear, which dominates the mine. Kits of mine buildings are less common. Some have been produced in brass, which are complicated but realistic, but others in card are less successful. It is possible to make a very convincing model coal mine using ready-made items, as long as you really go to town on the weathering. Coal dust was everywhere – not just on the mine buildings themselves, but on anything within reach of the mine.

A mine is also a great excuse for modelling small Coal Board locomotives as well as, for example, using the excellent J94 models of Hornby and DJ Models.

Other dominant industrial buildings seen along the London Midland Region are factories and mills. Many of the mills are now used for other purposes, but many more were still in full operation in the 1960s and 1970s.

Metcalfe make a large range of factory buildings that may be used to represent almost any type of industrial structure in either OO gauge or N gauge. They are easy to construct and to modify.

RAILWAY STRUCTURES

SIGNAL BOXES

Many of the older signal boxes found on most of the London Midland Region are of a similar type. For ease of construction, they were modular, using a few basic sections, which could be assembled into various sizes of box, according to the needs of the location. Depending on the original railway company that built the box, they might still have looked quite different (*see* Chapter 1). Generally, the higher the number of points and signals that needed operating, the larger the box was built.

One of the earliest models of a suitable signal box was the Oakham box, produced by Airfix back in the 1950s and still available in the Dapol range. It is a good basic model, which may be easily made more convincing by replacing the original window sections with those available from Ratio models. The Ratio model itself is of a two-bay signal box. It too can be easily modified by adding part of a second kit, to create a three-bay version. A new roof may be made from plastic tile sheets from the Wills range.

A Churchward Models brass kit of a two-bay box, which stands at Darley Green station on the Famous Trains layout. It is not for beginners! The two model signals are a LMS upper quadrant tubular post on the left and a MR lower quadrant on the right.

The larger three-bay signal box at Chinley station. The basis is the two-bay Ratio box, extended with plasticard and re-roofed with Wills plastic. It is represented in the run-down condition in which it would have been seen in the 1950s, with no balcony.

IMPROVING A BASIC MODEL SIGNAL BOX

The Airfix/Dapol signal box model was introduced in the 1950s/60s, based on the Midland box at Oakham in Rutland. Considering the age of the kit, it is still a nice little model, and a lot cheaper than the more recent kits. It is straightforward to improve with the aid of Midland windows, which are available in plastic from Ratio Models and as laser-cut items in wood fibre from Model Railway Scenery, for example. A few odds and ends of plastic and wire are also needed.

First, remove the centre bars from each of the three windows in the upper front wall section. File the openings lightly so that the larger Ratio windows will fit inside, then glue them in place. Glaze them with the clear plastic supplied.

The windows in the end walls are oversize, but can be improved by using microstrip to make glazing bars. The best way to do this is to fit the glazing on the inside of the wall, then carefully cut and fit the glazing bars on to the glazing. The door may be glazed in the same way.

Assemble the rest of the model as instructed, using the original windows and doors where required. However, you might prefer to fit the lower-floor window on the inside, again removing the glazing bars and replacing them with microstrip. Before the roof is fitted, you need to decide whether the interior is to be detailed. If not, you should still put in a floor made from card or plastic, and give the inside a coat of paint. The large windows allow plenty of the interior to be viewed.

If you do decide to detail the interior, suitable kits are available in plastic and metal from Ratio and Springside Models, and more recently from Metcalfe in a laser-cut version. These can really enhance the appearance of a model.

One feature missing from the basic model is the railing around the platform below the windows. If you are modelling during the later period of British Railways, these railings were often damaged or completely missing. If you want to represent the railings, you can use either plastic rod, with a diameter of about 0.5mm, or similar-gauge brass rod, if you wish to solder. In the pictures, metal rod is used for the handrail, bent to shape, and ABS rod for the uprights. These are fitted into holes drilled into the plastic platform around the box. Superglue fixes it all together.

Once it has been painted in colours that are appropriate for the LM Region, you will have a quite convincing model of a signal box for about £14.

(continues overleaf)

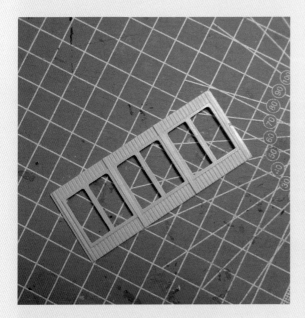

The upper front wall before modifying.

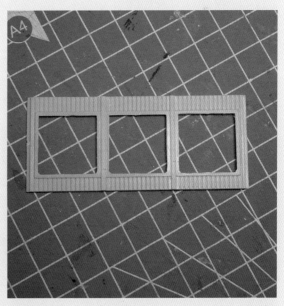

Centre window bars removed.

Ratio windows fitted after a little filing.

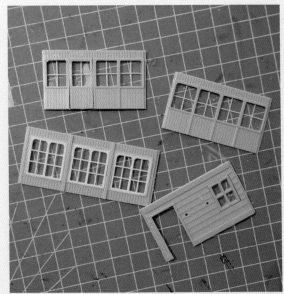

Glazing bars fitted in end windows and lower window.

LEFT: **The basic box assembled and glazed.**

BELOW: **White-metal rod railing added, with plastic rod uprights glued together and the stairs added.**

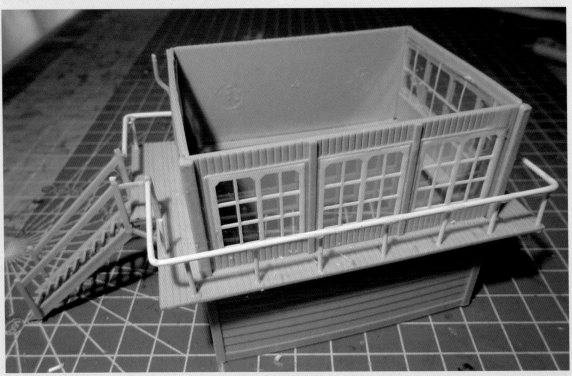

The roof is completed. The floor and interior detail should be added at this stage, and the inside painted before fixing the roof on.

The completed box, painted ready to set in place.

The real Oakham signal box today.

Metcalfe signal box based on a LNWR design.

A very detailed brass model of a similar box is also made by Churchward Models (CM44), although this is one for experienced users of a soldering iron.

Hornby produced a limited-edition resin model of the box at Barrow Hill. This is an accurate model, but may be a bit hard to find.

A sizeable part of the London Midland Region was, before 1923, the London North Western Region, which provided routes to the North West and into North Wales. The LNWR had its own style of signal box, one of which is produced by Metcalfe Models as a strong and realistic card model that lends itself to extra detailing. It is available in both OO and N gauge. For 7mm modellers, there are several LNWR boxes in the Rail Model range. A downloadable version in all three scales is available of the box at Hartington, once on the Cromford

and High Peak Railway. Finally, London Road Models make a brass kit of a LNWR Type 4 box that can be modified into the later Type 5 box.

LINESIDE FENCING – STATION AREAS

The Midland Railway developed a distinctive style of fencing. It used vertical posts, with horizontal rails, but, instead of vertical palings, it was fixed at an angle of about 30 degrees to the vertical. This style of fencing was used on platforms and in the close areas to stations and yards, as shown in model form in the picture of Chinley signal box.

It was normally painted a dark brown colour, probably using a tar-based paint, although some examples of white-painted fencing have appeared on some preservation sites.

The ubiquitous Dapol (ex-Airfix) fencing. Standard post and rail fencing was used alongside track away from station areas.

Ratio produce this fencing in OO gauge in either brown or white. Peedie models produce similar fencing in N gauge.

Away from station areas, the lineside fencing in the LM Region is much the same as anywhere else, being post and rail or post and wire in construction.

FOOTBRIDGES

Footbridges on the LM Region varied very much from place to place, with styles remaining from the pre-grouping companies, such as the LNWR and MR. In general, most were of a lattice-in-frame type, using either metal columns from the ground

The footbridge at Chinley station is constructed from three Hornby kits so as to cross four running lines. The steps are omitted and the span sits on two stone piers. The steps were re-used to allow access down the embankment (right) and down to the ground to the left of the bridge.

or platform, or stone-built piers when building out from embankments or over a longer span. Many were painted in a distinctive mix of red and cream, echoing the colours used on the station buildings. The framework was in red and the lattice infilling was cream. Supporting columns were often red, although some were black.

A good representation of such a bridge may be made from the Hornby kit No. R076, which is made in a soft, flexible green plastic that clips together. It may be easily adapted by combining with a second kit, to span four or more tracks. If this is to be done, a superglue is best for assembling it. The bridge at Chinley (*see* previous page) was constructed from three such kits, but required strengthening along its length with a thin metal strip from an old Venetian blind. Because of the nature of the plastic, it is wise to prepare the completed model with a plastic primer, otherwise the paint will not adhere.

CONSTRUCTING A LASER-CUT FOOTBRIDGE

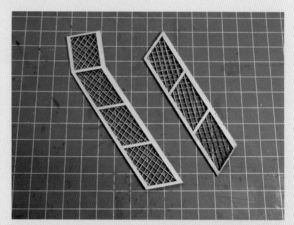

Once you have identified all the parts, and read the instructions, cut out the parts you need using a sharp knife. File the cut edges with an emery board or file to get a smooth surface.

The railings are very fine, so take great care in cutting them from the sprue. The frame is separate from the mesh, so carefully stick the frame over the mesh, ensuring the edges are all straight and smooth. Remember to make mirror images of each part so that the frame is always on the outside! You will not be able to separate them once assembled. Use a PVA glue with a fine applicator for the best results.

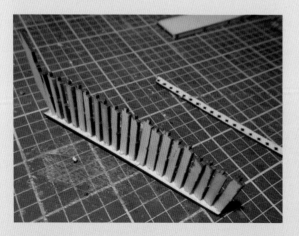

Assembling the steps requires patience and a steady hand. Use a fine wire or thin piece of plastic to put the glue into the holes before using tweezers to place each step in turn. They will seem uneven at first, but once the second side is fitted they will straighten up. Make sure they sit at the same angle before the glue dries. Keep the stair sections on a flat surface until they dry.

Recent developments in laser-cutting have created the opportunity for highly detailed models of structures such as bridges. One lovely example is LCUT's model of a London Midland Railway footbridge, which is straightforward to make (see below).

WATER COLUMNS/CRANES

The earlier companies that became the London Midland Region all had their own distinctive types of water column or crane, both platform- and ground-based. The Midland varieties are available as models from Mike's Models and Duncan's Models as white-metal kits in both OO and O gauge. LNWR varieties are available from the same sources.

STATION BUILDINGS

Each of the pre-grouping companies of the LMS and London Midland Region had their own style of station building (see Chapter I), and stations along

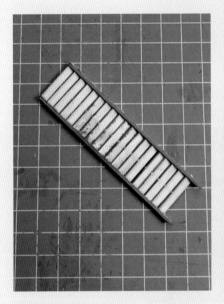

There are four sections with steps, so make them all so they can dry before assembly. Make sure that each one is square and flat.

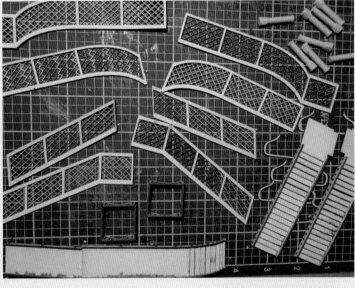

The railings are attached to the sides of the stair and top sections. Once you have assembled all the basic sections, the railings, the steps and the column supports, you can start assembling the bridge.

Assemble the bridge top first, following the instructions. The top sections fit end to end, but you need to cut off the end upright of one pair of the railings so that all the uprights match in size. Then add the stairs and their railings. When joining the parts, keep them supported, again giving the glue time to dry. Finally, add the column supports and the columns. The finished bridge is strong enough but very light in weight.

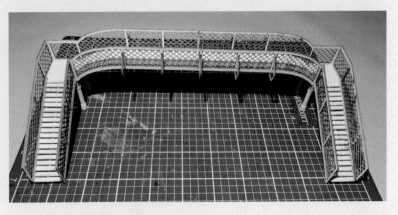

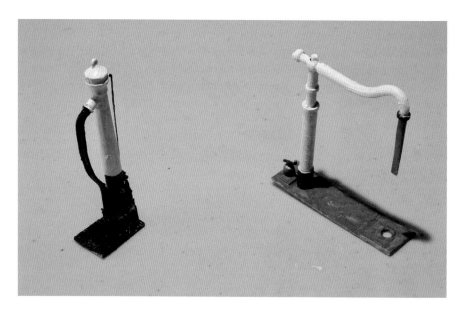

A London Midland Region water column by Skytrex and a London Midland Region water crane by P and D Marsh.

certain routes often had common features. The buildings at the small through stations on the line from Sheffield to Manchester, for example, were often constructed of a stone base with a timber-framed, single-storey structure above, topped with a slate roof. Stations at Hathersage and Grindleford follow this example. Others, such as that which stood at Chinley, an important junction on the same line, were quite different. The main building had a stone lower floor but the upper floor, which led to the footbridge access, looked like a half-timbered building with black-painted timber frame and white-painted infill. The rooms beneath the canopies were standard stone and timber structures used across the Region, but the restaurant looked more like a detached house!

A busy day at Chinley station, with Sheffield-bound Midland Compound 41154.
C.M. AND J.M. BENTLEY

The same view of Chinley station, this time on the Famous Trains layout.

The best way to reflect these variations accurately, if you plan to model a specific location, is to visit it and take pictures if you can, or do as much research as possible by studying old photographs.

The more important the station, the bigger the building is likely to be. The larger the building, the stronger it should be built, with good internal bracing.

If the model represents a fictional place, many of the card kits are excellent value, although the buildings may not necessarily be found on the London Midland Region. Metcalfe offer a range of models to make up a large through station or terminus. They may be fitted together in a number of configurations to create what is required. They have also just introduced a range of station buildings based on those on the Settle to Carlisle line, which are appropriate for this part of the London Midland Region. The kits make up into very realistic models that may be easily adapted.

Metcalfe's card model of a Settle and Carlisle station.

The Midland-style running-in boards on Chinley station platform. These were replaced by flat boards during the 1950s, which were plainer but retained the same colours.

PLATFORM FEATURES

A number of features on the station platform will also identify a model as being London Midland. The station name boards and running-in boards should be coloured in the crimson red of the Region, with white lettering. Platform number boards on the station, door plates, door frames and the doors themselves should also follow the same colour scheme. In BR days, the colours were standardized.

The lamp standards on platforms are distinctive of the Region and still reflected the original line builders from before grouping in 1923. Gas lamps continued on platforms even after the creation of British Railways, but, from the 1950s, more modern lighting appeared, with concrete posts and better illumination. Small station name signs were often attached to lamp standards.

Lighting guidelines for the LM Region were laid out in a detailed design handbook, which illustrated examples of the fittings to be used. Earlier platform lighting was of the incandescent type; the typical fitting and column are produced by Bachmann. Concrete lighting columns were replaced in the 1960s by steel columns, mainly of the hinged 'raise and lower' format. By the late 1960s, fluorescent fittings became the standard and the single-pole twin 40-watt and the post-top or under-canopy twin 65-watt fittings were common. Generally, the station name was inscribed on the diffuser. Yard lighting was also typical, with the Grenville light

London Midland Region pendant platform lights to pattern C on Bletchley station.

A rather forlorn F 6 pattern lamp standard.

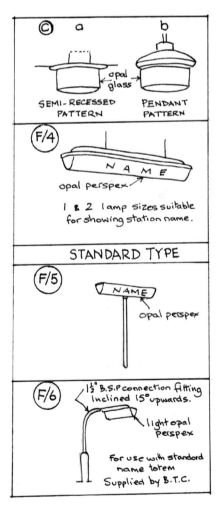

RIGHT: *The range of lights used on London Midland Region stations and platforms.*

MODIFYING A RESIN MODEL OF BUTTERLEY STATION

If you are not keen on building a station for yourself, one reasonable option is to use a ready-made structure such as Hornby's Skaledale model of Butterley station at the Midland Railway Centre (R9778). However, to make it really accurate, it will need some modifications. Reference to photographs of the real thing show that some features have been left unmodelled, or represented by two-dimensional images.

The rebuilt station at Butterley at the Midland Railway Centre is representative of many stations to be found on the London Midland Region. The original station was of identical design but was brick built. The rebuilt station was moved to its present site from Whitwell.

A close-up of the Butterley station doorway, with the slate roof removed.

Hornby's model of Butterley station as it comes out of the box, with the slated roof over the platform entrance.

The Hornby model at first sight is a well-detailed structure, but there are some unexpected variations, probably caused by attempts to keep production costs down. For example, the sloping pitch of the Italianate Victorian roof is shallower than it should be. To remedy this on the model would require major surgery and it would probably be better to start from scratch! However, other features are more easily corrected.

On the model, the sloping flat roof on the platform side of the building has been reproduced in tiles. This is in fact a glazed roof. It is a separate section, which may be removed by careful cutting with a fine saw, or repeated strokes with a sharp knife. The glazed supporting wall should be separated from the roof first. As the tiled roof is not required, it will not be a problem if this supporting wall is broken during the removal. At this time, it

is also necessary to remove the printed 'Butterley' name above the doors, which is incorrect.

A replacement roof may be constructed from a piece of rigid, clear plastic, with plasticard glazing bars and frame. The roof has a decorative steel girder across the front, which rests upon the pillars that once supported the tiled roof. Before refitting, it is a good idea to touch in the walls with matching paints as this will be difficult once the glazed section is in place. There is also a gutter along the front that links to a downpipe on the right-hand side, which is not modelled at all on Hornby's version. These, along with two other downpipes, may be easily added using proprietary plastic items available from either Ratio or Wills.

If you want to add some 'life' to the model, it is possible to remove the closed doors with a razor saw and replace them with card or plastic alterna-

The glazing fitted, new gutter and downpipe added and the correct name board in place.

The new firebuckets fitted and gas lamps in place.

The completed Butterley station, showing all the changes to the platform side. Now renamed 'Darley Green', it may be seen on the Famous Trains layout (see Chapter 2).

tives in the open position. Two further doors inside the glazed section are also omitted and may be added by mounting thin card doors on the surface.

The six hanging buckets on the platform side are moulded in place, but the red painted boards to which each set of three is mounted are not modelled. It is straightforward to carefully paint this on to the model wall, or, for greater realism, remove the buckets with a sharp knife and file and mount card or plastic boards to the walls. Because the resin is quite hard, a Dremel type of tool may be used to file away the old fire buckets.

New mounting panels are made from plasticard or thin card, painted red. Hanging brackets are made from fine track pins fixed into 0.5mm holes drilled into the station body. Fire buckets are available from many suppliers and these may be added. (Make this the last job before setting the model in place, as these small parts can easily fall off when being handled, and are far harder to fit back on once the model is in place.) On the model, the buckets are ready-painted items by Bachmann.

The station name board should read 'Butterley for Ripley and Swanwick'. It hangs from the front edge of the glass canopy and is simply made from a computer-printed paper, mounted on thin black card and held in place by two fine track pins glued to the glass roof. A look at photographs will show that the notice boards on the model are fitted incorrectly. It might be easiest to print these out on a computer and cover those already in place.

The window frames are painted all white, but it is clear from photographs of the real thing that they should be trimmed with a narrow maroon line round the edges. This may be re-created using a fine fibre-tipped pen.

Missing from the original model are two distinctive, delicate wall lamps, which have been added using two white-metal lamps from the Langley range.

If you wish to light the model, as the windows are quite large, it is worth modelling interior details. Colouring the walls helps to stop the light 'bleeding' through the resin from which the model is made. There are several downloadable options for creating interiors, or you can create your own with card or plastic sheet. Remember to keep the lighting dim, by fitting a resistor in the circuit, otherwise the model will look as if it has searchlights inside it!

It is worth looking over the whole model carefully once the modifications are complete, to see if you can spot and touch in any unpainted areas, behind downpipes for example.

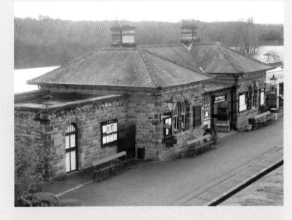

A picture of the real Butterley station at the Midland Railway Centre.

A London Midland Region platform seat at Oakham station. Note the chains to prevent it running away.

fitting on a medium size pole being standard. High lattice towers were used in all the West Coast marshalling yards and there was also an 'engine shed fitting' often found on building faces.

All station platforms would have outside seating for passengers. These seats usually reflected their company of origin, with cast or decorated end supports and wooden slats for the seat and back. Sometimes, the station name was painted on the upper back slat.

GOODS DEPOTS

Most stations had an associated goods depot. Generally, the larger and more important the station was, the larger and more important its depot. However, it may often have been no more than a single platform and covering shed with a road access to the side. There was less standardization with goods sheds, as they had to reflect the requirements of the town or village. Many were of simple

The small goods shed at Chinley on the Famous Trains layout.

wood design on a brick base built on to a platform of stone, brick or wood construction.

A simple way to construct such a shed is to use or modify a model in kit or ready-built form, but, as it is a basic shell, it is also straightforward to build from card or plastic, basing your design on a photograph. On the Chinley layout, strips of painted cartridge paper were used on a card shell to represent the goods shed.

More substantial depots were built of either local stone or, more likely, brick in larger towns and cities. They were often very large structures with several roads for the transfer of goods and would also have had yards for the storage of goods wagons outside as well.

Coal traffic rarely used depots such as these, the principal wagons being vans of various types. Coal, oil and quarry products, for example, were handled by specific depots, as specialized equipment was needed for their unloading and transfer.

HINTS AND TIPS

- Create a collection of photographs of the area you want to model. Take pictures not just of suitable buildings, but of the landscape too. Look online for other pictures, then you can be sure to have an accurate basis from which to work.
- Always keep leftover scraps of plastic, card or metal from kits. Spare windows are really useful, as are gutters and downpipes. Keep a stock of glazing material from packaging. Many card kits come with alternative doors and interiors, which can save a lot of time and effort.
- Try out different construction materials for buildings. Some people prefer mounting board, embossed card and brick or stone paper, while others prefer textured plastic sheet. Plastic is more expensive, so if you are a beginner and are worried about making mistakes, go for the card option. With brick papers, there is no need to paint the walls!

Equipment
- Cutting mat
- Steel rule
- Sharp pencil
- Newspaper
- Quick-setting filler (ready mixed)
- White glue (PVA)

- Plastic solvent/glue
- Superglue
- Patience

Toolbox and box of bits
- Scalpel or sharp snap-off knife
- 'Stanley' type knife
- Small files or sanding block
- Razor saw
- Dremel type rotary tool with abrasive discs
- Pin vice and 0.5mm drill bit
- Old paintbrushes for spreading glue

Materials
- Acrylic or enamel paints in correct BR colours
- Watercolour paints
- 5mm thick foamboard
- Mounting board (1mm thick)
- Window frames or microstrip
- Gutter and downpipe kit (Ratio, for example)
- Rigid clear plastic about 1mm thick
- 0.5mm plasticard
- 0.5mm diameter wire or plastic rod
- Fine track pins
- Expanded polystyrene packaging
- Proprietary 'water' kit or gloss varnish
- Suitable walling material in stone or brick
- Flock or grass scenic scatter for towpaths

CHAPTER SEVEN

SCENIC MODELLING

From the Midlands north, the higher land crossed by the London Midland Region required more engineering to pass through. Rocky cuttings are a feature of the Peak District and quarries could be found near to railways in many places. The North Wales coastal railway is often backed by steep sea cliffs and the lines across the limestone hills of the Pennines often had deep rocky cuttings.

MODELLING ROCK FEATURES AND STONE

Modelling rock is not as difficult as might be imagined. There are several ways of creating rocky landscapes, from using rubber moulds to cast rock faces, to layering materials with uneven edges to make a face and then covering with plaster and shaping with a knife. Ready-made rock faces are available and may be cut to fit the space you have. Some types of tree bark are suitable for creating rock faces. They may have to be coloured with paints, but some can look just right without modification.

Look at examples of rock faces near to the location that you are planning to model. They may appear layered if the rock is limestone or another sedimentary rock. If they are very fractured, the rock may well be harder, such as gritstone or even granite.

The most realistic faces may be made easily by casting a lightweight plaster in rubber moulds, such as those supplied by Woodland Scenics. Mix the plaster as recommended and pour into the moulds until they are filled. Keep them level and let them dry out thoroughly. If you try to take the plaster out too soon, it may well break. If it does, do not discard the pieces, as they may be useful.

Some very convincing rock faces constructed from tree bark collected from nearby woods. They have not been coloured in any way.

Once dry, the pieces may be removed by gently bending the mould to release the plaster.

The pieces may then be arranged on an embankment or base and moved around until a convincing arrangement is made. Refer regularly to photographs. Each piece may be fixed in place with a little more plaster, or even some PVA glue. Again, let it dry thoroughly.

When it comes to painting the rocks, do look at colour pictures before you start. It is very easy to assume that all rocks are grey! Coloured dyes are available from Woodland Scenics, but watercolour paints or very thinned acrylics are also suitable. Work from light to dark. An overall wash of a light base colour will hide all the white of the plaster. Near to the vegetation at the top or sides there may well be an area of browner tint, as the rock becomes soil. Large faces of rock will have subtle

Plaster castings fresh out of Woodland Scenics moulds.

Castings arranged on to a sloping bank and fixed in place with more plaster of Paris.

A light watercolour wash is used over the whole area and then varied colours are added to give depth.

Grass and vegetation are finally added to the rock face.

A railway cutting constructed using the casting technique.

variations in colour, which may be added by working on each area separately.

Where rock is deeply incised, or has cracks and fissures, a thin wash of much darker colour may be dribbled down from above. This will darken the crevices, highlight the texture of the rock and quickly bring the rock face to 'life'.

Once the rock face has dried, vegetation and other details may be added with flock or static grass.

The further north you travel on the LMR, the more likely you are to see fields and roads bordered by stone walls. Although there are local differences in the construction of stone walls, in model form they tend to look very similar. There are many options for adding stone walls to a layout, with

several varieties of resin construction and others cast from a hard plaster or plastic. In each case, it is important to blend the walling in by careful colouring and filling where each wall section joins the next.

Where walls run generally level, the ready-made ones look quite convincing, but stone walls often are constructed up and down steep hills. You may well have to cut the wall sections so that they follow the contours of the land. Luckily, the walls often have plenty of vegetation growing over them, so any gaps may be easily hidden with model foliage.

If you have the patience, really convincing stone walls can be made with small pieces of 'stone' made from broken-up excess plaster from moulding.

A stone wall assembled from commercial castings, weathered and bedded in with suitable vegetation.

A stone wall for the patient modeller. It has been assembled from individual stones, made from small chunks of plaster.

FARMLAND AND COUNTRYSIDE

Most modellers will not have enough space to model large areas of grassland on a layout, but, where it is done well, it can really enhance a model. Between London and the Midlands, the railway passes through vast areas of farmland linking numerous market towns. Fields are quite large and the later time period you model, the fewer the hedgerows. More modern farming machinery is more efficient in large fields.

From the Peak District northwards, fields are smaller, because of the steepness of the hills, and hedges give way to stone walls. Trees become scarcer and confined to valley areas. This continues into the Lake District and North Wales, where the land is highest.

Farmland is often greener than moorland, as it is cultivated. Treeless moorland is often a brownish-green in colour.

There are many tried and tested ways of creating grassland. One of the simplest is to build the shape of the land with expanded polystyrene or insulation material, then cover the surface with strips of newspaper pasted over each other. Allow the structure to dry, then paint it a brown colour and cover it with PVA glue. One of the many varieties of scatter material can then be sieved over the surface to make the grass. Blending the scatter material helps to show the variety of colours in a field.

Larger areas, or tunnels, may be made in a similar way, except that the base is made from a framework of card or light wood, covered with a woven surface of cereal packet strips before covering with the newspaper strips. Grass mats may also be used, although they are often a bit too uniform in colour and texture, and sometimes difficult to form to the shape of the landscape

With the use of static grass, an even more real-

The woven card method of constructing scenery. This area covers four main-line running tracks so it is important to have plenty of clearance, which the woven method allows.

A completed section of countryside with static grass in the foreground. The locomotive is a London Midland Region 3F Jinty by Bachmann.

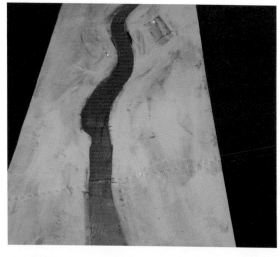

The development of the scenic part of the layout featuring the Jinty. The land is formed with layers of foamboard, covered with paper and painted.

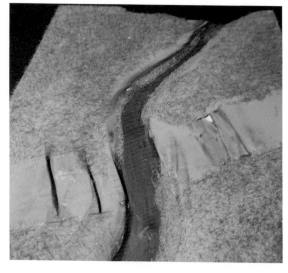

An initial layer of static grass is applied and allowed to dry.

ABOVE: **The bridge is in place and several more layers of static grass are added, along with foliage round the bridge and sand along the river bed.**

The river 'water' has been added, along with reeds and stones and boulders. Longer static grass has also appeared.

istic grass surface can be achieved. An easy way to improve on existing scatter-covered fields, or grass mat, is to apply PVA glue over the surface where you want and then use a static grass applicator to cover everything with a layer of static grass. Further layers of static grass can be built up, using hairspray as a fixative, rather than glue. This creates a wide range of textures and colours to enhance the scene.

Where land is used for arable farming – as in the parts of the London Midland Region between London and the Midlands – fields are often ploughed. Again, there are several methods of producing this in model form. A good representation of a ploughed field can be created by using a piece of corduroy or needlecord fabric (brown is ideal), cut to size and glued down to the surface. It can then be painted

with a mixture of earth tones and blended into the surrounding area by using scatter or static grass.

Lengths of thick string may be stuck down next to each other and painted for creating a smaller area or a field being ploughed. Another method is to use a thin mix of plaster, spread over the area to be shown as ploughed and then carefully 'combed' with an old comb with some teeth removed. Once dry, this may be painted in the same way as before.

It is rare that there will be enough space on a model to create a complete farm, but a range of farm buildings is essential to set the scene. These may be scratch-built or based on real examples, or made from the wide range of kit models available, for example, in card from Metcalfe and Superquick, in laser-cut MDF from Petite Properties, or in

A ploughing demonstration at Chinley Farm. The ploughed area is represented by combed plaster.

A Petite Properties model farmhouse – an MDF shell, covered with plaster, scribed and painted.

plastic from Dapol, Faller or Noch. Very convincing stone structures are provided by Townstreet Models in plaster.

Whatever method is chosen, any model will be greatly improved by looking at pictures of buildings in the area being modelled and applying 'weathering' to reflect the often grubby nature of a farmyard.

Any area of countryside will have plenty of hedging or trees. There are many excellent ready-made models of both hedges and different types of trees, to allow quick 'forestation'. Creating your own trees is time-consuming, although very rewarding. Use wire armatures for the framework and cover with a paste or PVA and powdered filler

Chinley Farm model, created from several Townstreet plaster kits, painted and weathered.

MODELLING A CANAL AND LOCK

Once drawn out on the baseboard, the canal sides may be built up with expanded polystyrene, or any suitable material, to a thickness of about 8mm. Where the lock is to be placed, the depth of the sides may be increased with thicker layers.

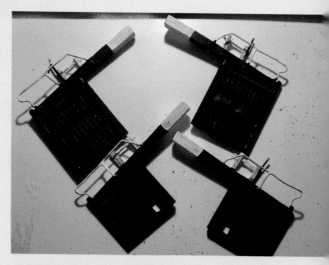

The canal sides may be covered with a suitable textured finish, in this case, pre-coloured textured stone card by Metcalfe models. Coping stones have been added using scribed card, and recesses have been built to allow the lock gates to fit.

A set of Langley white-metal lock gates, for a wide lock, assembled, primed and then painted with acrylic paints.

On this section of canal, a different method of constructing the sides is used, with small regular pieces of plaster being laid to represent stones in the canal walls. The canal base has been covered with pasted paper to provide a smooth surface and the coping stones on the wall are small separate tiles.

The canal bed has now been painted with murky brown and green colours and the towpaths have been given a basic coat of landscaping materials.

LEFT: *A Craftline single lock in place. The gates are fixed in the open position as if a boat is about to enter or leave the lock. Note that the scenery has been completed near to the canal, which now awaits paper and paint on the lock floor.*

Once the area has been cleaned of loose scatter materials, the canal may be filled with 'water'. This is a two-part resin material, which takes about forty-eight hours to harden. It is self-levelling so it is important to ensure there is nowhere for it to drain away. Once the resin has hardened, any weeds may be added, being attached with PVA glue. Further detailing may be carried out, as the hardened water is easy to keep clean.

to make the bark. Paint and then, when dry, use suitable foliage materials to finish. Once again, there are many excellent articles available on the different ways to model realistic trees.

MODELLING WATER

CANALS

One very important feature of the London Midland Region is the large number of canals that criss-cross the area. A canal always makes an interesting feature on a layout, whether it is in the countryside or in an urban setting. In 1948 the canal system was nationalized, along with the railways, and often BR ran the railway links to the inland canal ports, thus creating an interesting modelling example.

Canals are quite straightforward to model as the water does not flow like a river, so there is no need to represent any ripples! Canal banks are usually near-vertical and were constructed from what-ever local materials were available – stone, brick,

wooden baulks, and so on. Old rails are often to be seen reinforcing canal banks.

The most interesting features of canals are the locks, with their wooden gates. These may be scratch-built for a model from balsa wood, or assembled from white-metal kits from suppliers such as Langley, who make both single- and double-gate versions. Craftline also make excellent balsa kits of lock gates, bridges and narrow boats.

Locks were constructed to raise or lower boats when the canal encountered a change in land level, so model canals and locks must also follow the lie of the land. Lock gates close by water pressure, so it is important to ensure that the vee shape made by the gates points towards the higher level of water.

A number of interesting structures were also built where canals and railways met, in order to transfer goods from boat to rail and vice versa. The structure on the Cromford canal was used for that purpose and the model (see below) shows it as it once was.

A model of the exchange shed on the Cromford canal, prior to being finished. The model is constructed of foamboard, with a covering of horizontal strips of cartridge paper to represent the stone courses. The vertical joints are created with a sharpened screwdriver.

RIVERS

When you approach the modelling of a river, whether small or large, you will soon appreciate the advantages of an open-framed baseboard. As long as it is planned for, creating a lower river section is straightforward. The important thing is to ensure that you have a well-supported track bed, which can become your embankment and bridge or viaduct. It is then simple to fit a lower board at the point where you want to have the river scene.

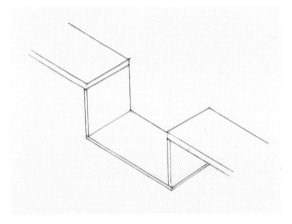

Baseboard with lower section in place prior to constructing the track bed and bridge.

If you are modelling a deeper river valley, it may be easier to model the whole section in situ. Start by creating a lower section of baseboard, then build the track bed across from one side to the other. This needs to be the width of the bridge you are going to build. Construct vertical supports where the bridge arches will be, so that the track is well supported down to the lower baseboard. At this stage, it is worth creating the bridge itself, using a kit or designing your own. As the structure is already strong, you may make the bridge quite light, using card or sheet plastic.

Fill in the valley using layers of polystyrene foam or any other landscaping method, such as woven strips of card over formers. Make sure you leave a channel for your river and then cover the whole scenic section with newspaper strips, fixed with diluted PVA glue.

Once it has hardened, the surface can be covered with brown paint, to seal the surface, and grass and ground cover may be added using suitable scatter material or static grass, again fixed with PVA. The river is then detailed with stones, sand and gravel and reeds, available from companies such as Woodland Scenics and Javis. As a rule, banks

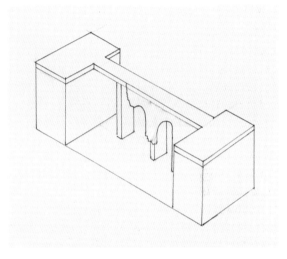

The track bed in place, with the bridge supports erected and work begun on cladding the bridge with arches.

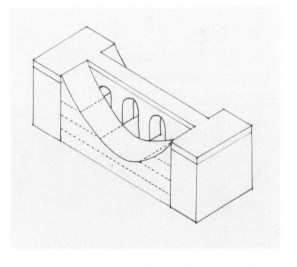

The bridge is complete and the valley contours have been added with layers of expanded polystyrene, covered with pasted paper. Once everything is dry, the process of using scatter and foliage can be started.

A girder bridge constructed across a valley, which has been made as described above. The rock details are castings made from Woodland Scenics moulds. The locomotive is a Midland Railway 7F 53810 by Bachmann, which would have run on the Somerset & Dorset Joint Railway.

are steeper on the outside of river bends and shallower on the inside, so any sand will be visible on the inside of a bend.

At this stage, you can glue in any reeds or waterside plants you wish to add, unlike where you are modelling the still water of a canal. River water is flowing, so you may well want to add ripples and small waves, and adding plants is more difficult once the waves are set.

You can use paints to enhance your rivers by deepening the colour towards the centre of the stream and by adding white around rocks to show foam and spray.

There are a number of readily available products for creating rivers and water effects. Do some research on what they are best for, as some have specific properties for waves and others for smooth water.

A river on the Famous Trains model railway, showing the effect of moving water, which may be achieved by using the special types of model water.

CHAPTER EIGHT

SIGNALLING

Many railway modellers miss out on providing signals on their model railways, for a number of reasons. Some people just do not understand signalling – which signals should go where on a layout, or even whether signals are required at all, for example, at a small village terminus. Also, which signals are appropriate to the era you are modelling? It is a potential minefield if realism is needed and, if you get it wrong, there will always be another modeller who will come along and say, usually loudly so that other people can hear, 'That's not right.'

This chapter aims to explain first what signals should go where on a model railway, separating them into semaphore signals and electric light signals (colour light, multiple-aspect and the like). Second, it will illustrate some of the types that were widely used on the Midland Region. Third, it will describe the products that are available to buy commercially, both ready-made and in kit form, in particular for OO scale.

SEMAPHORE SIGNALLING

SIGNALLING SYSTEMS

When railways were in their infancy, back in the early nineteenth century, the process for despatching trains from a station was usually based on the

The signals on the gantry at the end of Trent station platform are former Midland Railway lower quadrant semaphores, still in use on 28 April 1962. They act as starters for the platform, the passenger loop line, and the first goods loop. The starter for the second goods loop is the LMS tubular post upper quadrant signal at the left edge of the four tracks. 8F 2-8-0 48079 is passing with a loaded coal train.

Stanier Class 5 4-6-0 No. 44966 starts away from Skipton with a northbound stopping train on 20 April 1957. The starter signal has a repeater arm high up above the normal arm, so that the signal can be seen above the station buildings from a train approaching the station from the south. A repeater arm always shows the same aspect as the main signal. These are LMS upper quadrant signals on a square post.

'time-interval' system. This was fine when everything was working right, which it usually did if the time intervals were set sufficiently far apart. However, if a train broke down, or a locomotive ran out of steam, for example, there was no protection to prevent the following train from running into the back of the train that had stopped on the running line.

In the decades since the railways began to have major train crashes, the Government issued legislation that forced the railway companies to set up signalling systems that would keep trains apart from each other when out on the running lines. The key principle adopted was 'space interval'. By dividing the running lines into 'block sections', in each of which only one train could run at a time, the trains could be kept apart from each other. Each block

section was controlled by a signalman (nowadays called a 'signaller', because the individual can be male or female) in a cabin, colloquially known as a signal box. To a large extent, all the signalling systems that are capable of being modelled are based on the block system. Only the very modern train-borne systems do not use lineside signals. Their introduction to normal railways will be half a century after BR and the Midland Region disappeared, so it is not relevant here.

On a traditional semaphore-signalled railway, each block section begins near and in the sight of a signaller in a signal box. The normal sequence of signals that the signaller controls begins with a 'distant' signal, usually quite a long way before an oncoming train reaches the signal box, and often out of sight from the 'box. That signal has an arm

Peak No. D65 approaches Kettering station with a Bradford–London St Pancras express on 28 April 1962. In the right background is the junction bracket signal; the route is set for the diversion from the straight route on to the adjoining main line, so the lower signal arms are at clear for this manoeuvre. The nearby signal almost alongside the locomotive is at danger, as D65's move across the layout is a confliction.

with a 'fishtail' cut into the outer the end; in the UK the side that faces oncoming trains is painted yellow with a black stripe that is also fishtail-shaped. The back side of the arm is white with a black fishtail stripe. A train can pass a distant signal whatever its aspect, because, if the signal is showing a 'caution' aspect (with the arm at 90 degrees to its post), it is advising the driver that one or more of the other signals in the section ahead is at danger and he or she must proceed with caution to see what the next signal is showing.

The next signal that the train reaches is normally

A former LNWR electric unit arrives at Dalston junction on a Broad Street–Richmond working on 29 March 1958. The electrification here was laid with four rails -- two running and two earth – to conform with London Underground's system, along which this train would travel on the Richmond branch. The starter signal (extreme left) has a white diamond to indicate that a train standing at the signal is detected by track circuits.

On this model of Chinley station, the left bracket signal is set for straight ahead; this arm is higher than the one that would indicate diversion to the line heading off right. This bracket signal's base will eventually be buried under the platform surface and the operating wires made less visible. The other pair of bracket signals that control the exit from the bay platform are of the same height, indicating routes of equal status.

An LMS tubular post upper quadrant starter (left), with the distant arm for the next section below it. Note the position of the white diamond – below the starter to which it refers and above the next section's distant. 4F 0-6-0 44400 is approaching Colne in east Lancashire from the Accrington direction.

the 'home' signal. The arm of any stop signal, such as a home signal, is painted red with a white vertical stripe on the side facing an oncoming train. The back of the arm is white with a black vertical stripe. The home signal is usually within the sight of the signaller.

The home signal enables the signaller to stop the train if there is an obstruction ahead, such as another train stopped on the same line at a station platform, for example, or when shunting is in progress in the section. To stop a train, the signal must be set in the 'on' position, which has the signal arm at 90 degrees to the post, parallel to the ground. If the line is clear, that signal can be set in the 'off' position, which sets the arm at a 45-degree angle. It is angled downwards if it is a lower quadrant signal (the old-fashioned sort, with which the GWR persisted right up to and after nationalization), and upwards on an upper quadrant signal, which is the more common way. If the home signal is 'off', the train can proceed to the next signal, which in a simple block section will be the 'starter'. The starter signal is important because it enables the signaller to hold a train in section until the signaller controlling the next section has confirmed that that section is ready to accept the train. Traditionally, the signallers communicate with each other quickly using a bell code and block instruments to ensure signals are cleared before the train

appears; slow release of signals can delay a train unnecessarily.

Where a block section is particularly long, there is sometimes an additional home signal, which is called the 'outer home', placed well before the home signal is reached. This enables the signaller to hold a train there, to give space for other train or shunting moves to be made within the section. Also there can be an 'advance starter' to enable the signaller to hold a train beyond the starter signal ('in advance'), so that the signaller can accept another train into the section, maybe to stop at a platform without delaying it. But the advance starter must remain at danger (in other words, 'on') until the next section's signaller has accepted the train. Also, it is perfectly reasonable for the next section's distant signal to share the same post as the nearby section's starter or advance starter. In this case, the distant arm is placed below the stop signal arm.

In modelling terms, these signals are all set on a simple vertical post. They are ideal for a model of a through station where there are no junctions involved, either on the layout or theoretically beyond it. Where the line is double-tracked for Up and Down trains, left-hand running is the norm in the UK. The signals protecting the Up and Down lines are laid out as described in the above paragraphs, with the signals usually on the left of the running line.

If there is a junction anywhere on the layout, or beyond it in the modeller's mind, the divergence must be protected with two signals, usually set together on a bracket. If the two lines beyond the junction are of equal priority, the two signal posts are the same height and the signals are alongside each other at the same height. If the line ahead is the main line and the diverging route to one side or the other is a branch line, the main-line post is taller than that carrying the branch-line signal, so the main-line signal arm, being higher, is more prominent. A bracket can protect several divergences, and the number and layout of signal posts on the bracket make it clear to a train driver which line is set for the train to proceed.

In some yards and stations, several divergences have been signalled using multiple signal arms on one post, one above the other. The convention with this method is that the top signal reads 'first left' and the bottom one 'last right'. The others in between indicate routings moving across from left to right in the direction of travel. It is not as clear as using bracket signals, and out of favour for that reason.

Sometimes, a bracket signal group can carry a signal sending a train into a siding or a side loop line. This will usually be a signal with a short post and a short arm. The LM Region painted these red with a vertical white stripe, just like a normal stop signal arm. As with single-post signals, on a bracket a distant signal arm for the section ahead can be

Midland compound 4-4-0 41094 rolls into Skipton on 20 April 1957 with an excursion from Bradford to Southport, formed of a mixture of LMS and Midland Railway non-corridor stock. The bracket signals controlling its arrival stand on a Midland Railway lattice post, but the signals themselves are LMS upper quadrants on tubular posts. The short arm on the left diversion post is a calling-on arm, allowing a second train to enter the platform with another train already there.

A heavy double-headed limestone train climbs away from Tunstead quarry in Derbyshire in 1988. The locomotives are 45034 and 47258. The bracket signal on the left is an LMS tubular post example, with the main signals offset for ease of sighting. Note the guy rope tied to the bracket and embedded at the other end into the embankment.

LMS tubular-post bracket signal on the OO scale Darley Green branch at Famous Trains, made up from a Ratio kit. The main, high arm is Darley Green home and leads to the main platform; the right-hand, lower signal leads to the bay platform and the left short arm controls access to the goods yard.

carried on the same post as a stop signal, just below it.

Shunting within a section is under the control of the signaller where that activity can get in the way of trains running on the running lines. Within yards that have hand points, there is no need for ground signals as the signaller is not involved. A ground signal would be located at, for example, the exit from a yard, siding or loop to a main line, or at specific places on the running lines to enable shunting

There are many locations where signals are not easily sighted by train drivers. This 4F on a stopping train from Derby to Manchester in 1962 is approaching a disc repeater that shows the aspect of the Millers Dale Down home signal, which is out of view round a bend. The circular disc is white with a black stripe, which represents the position of the out-of-sight starter signal.

On 1 August 1959, a former L&YR electric unit approaches Bury Bolton Street on the side-contact third rail system that was replaced by Manchester Metrolink in 1992. The tall bracket signal (left background) is Bury's advance starter that also carries the next signal box's distant beneath it. The very short post on the left of the bracket has a short-arm stop signal that controls the entrance to Bury electric traction depot.

manoeuvres to take place that cannot be controlled using the main-line signals. Ground signals have white discs with a horizontal red line painted across the middle on the side facing a locomotive or train.

LM REGION SEMAPHORE TYPES: MODELS AVAILABLE

While the Midland Railway, the LNWR and the other smaller pre-grouping railways had their own styles of lower quadrant semaphore signals, the LMS standardized on a straightforward design of tubular-post upper quadrant signal. This can be found almost anywhere on the former LMS lines where there is still semaphore signalling in use, so even a modern image model railway based on the LMR can use these signals, as well as model railways set during the LMS period.

Happily, the most readily available model signals, for OO scale at least, are of this type. Dapol and Ratio produce ready-made single-post signals to the LMS tubular-post design, either worked electrically (Dapol) or manually through a lever arrangement in the signal post's base (Ratio). In addition to these, Ratio has a range of plastic kits of LMS tubular-post signals, as well as other types, including LNWR square-post signals. Model Signal Engineering (MSE) also offer LMS tubular-post signals and, in addition, Midland Railway lower quadrant signals with

wooden posts, and early LMS lattice-post signals. Similar signal kits are available for N and O gauges, too.

The Ratio kits are plastic and a little fragile, but with care they can be made up into very realistic and detailed signals, including bracket signals. They can be assembled with fully working parts, but they do demand a competent level of modelling skill to get them right. On a layout where working signals are not essential they can be assembled more easily without all the pull wires, but with everything glued in place. They will look very convincing from a normal viewing distance, even though they are fixed. Most of the signals around the Chinley layout at Famous Trains are made in this way, positioned with the main-line signals 'off', and there have been no comments from visitors that they do not appear to be working. Each Ratio bracket signal kit includes parts for two or three signal assemblies as well as four ground signals. These kits are extremely good value for money.

MSE kits are metal, not plastic, and so are higher up the ladder of 'skills required'. They make up into robust models and are therefore possibly a better choice for working model signals that are to be operated frequently over a long period. That said, there is a bracket signal from a Ratio plastic kit at Darley Green on the Famous Trains model railway.

How long it will last remains to be seen, but so far it has coped well with being hammered as part of an automatic train shuttle at the Darley Green terminus.

On a railway with seasonal or occasional traffic, or where there are regular but long periods with low traffic levels, the real railway has a system whereby a signal box can be 'switched out'. Before the signaller leaves the signal box, the signallers in the two 'boxes either side of the closing 'box must link their communications together, by-passing the closing signal box. The signaller must set all the running-line signals in the 'off' position, and then immediately send a bell code to the signal boxes on either side to indicate that the signal box is switching out. On a model railway, having a switched-out signal box enables a small layout to have signals in place that do not need to work, because they are always set in the 'off' position. The same can apply to a branch-line terminus where only one train is in use (the 'one engine in steam' principle).

SEMAPHORE SIGNALS ON A MODEL RAILWAY

On a model railway based on a main-line station, it is likely that the modeller will need to place home and starter signals on each running line. There can be a home signal some distance before, or even close to, the approach to each platform and a starter on or soon after each platform end. The starter signal may have a distant signal on the same post, if this makes sense following the general principles of semaphore signalling. Unless there is a junction somewhere, that is all that is needed on a simple two-track layout, or even on a single track if there is no loop. The latter will not necessarily need any signals at all. Where there is a passing loop on a model single-track line, if the two running lines between the loop points are uni-directional (in other words, trains always adopt left-hand running to call at the platforms), the signalling arrangement is the same as for a double-track line. The starter signal must be far enough back from the loop points to prevent a stopped train

A Class 123 DMU on a Hull to Manchester Piccadilly working passes Earl's sidings at Hope in Derbyshire on 18 April 1984. The signal on a tubular post (right) has a short stop arm, to enable a train from the cement works to enter BR property and sidings. The ground signal has two discs, one above the other, the upper one indicating a move to the left and the lower one to the right at the next sets of facing points.

from fouling the route of a train that is approaching from the opposite direction.

If the loop tracks are bi-directional – that is to say, trains can run on them in either direction – the home signals need to be bracket signals, normally of equal priority. In this instance, there needs to be a starter signal at each end of each platform before the tracks converge; on a wide island platform these can be single-post signals, but if an island platform end is narrow, a bracket signal can be used to carry the two starters side by side. Usually, distant signals on a model railway are not needed, due to the restricted length of the running lines. If a distant signal is needed (for example, to warn of an imaginary block section ahead that is not actually on the model railway), this can be on the post of each starter signal; again, the distant arm must be below the starter arm on the bracket concerned.

A simple double-track station on a model railway, with no loops, crossovers or sidings, can get away without any signals at all, based on the assumption that the station is in the middle of a long section that

is controlled from signal boxes at locations further up and down the line.

Where there are sidings off a running line, or a crossover, or a run-round loop, these can be signalled just with ground signals. These should be placed where the model driver of a train or locomotive can easily see them, in such a way as to cover every likely movement to or from or between the running lines. Because they are so small, model ground signals can sensibly be non-working, as no one will notice that the discs do not move! However, this arrangement requires a starter signal, or advance starter, beyond the points out of the yard so that the signaller can hold the train if the next section is not ready to receive the train. The alternative is to have a normal stop signal acting as a starter signal at the yard exit. There are also a few yellow ground signals with a black band across the disc. When one of these is 'on', it indicates that a shunt move can take place into a head-shunt and can pass the signal. The yellow ground signal is only 'off' if the points beyond it are set for a move out of the yard to the running line.

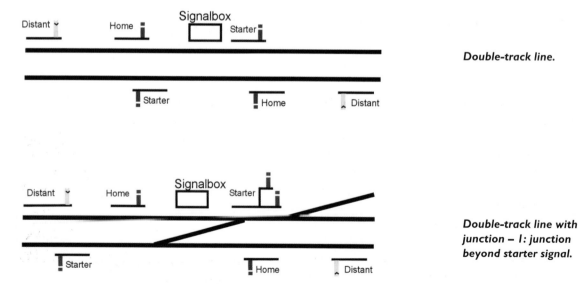

Double-track line.

Double-track line with junction – 1: junction beyond starter signal.

NB: There would also be distant and home signals on the branch line approach as shown in the top figure on the opposite page, and possibly also advance starters on the main line and branch line beyond the junction.

Double-track line with junction – 2: junction before starter signal.

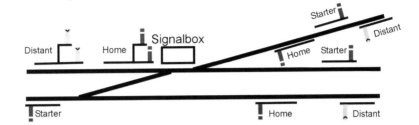

Single-track line with passing loop – uni-directional.

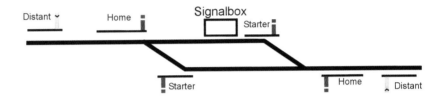

Single-track line with passing loop – bi-directional.

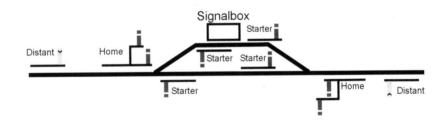

In both the loops shown above, there would also be a set of trap points at each of the loop outlets. These would divert runaway trains away from oncoming traffic on the main running line.

At the buffer stops at all platforms at a terminus station, or at the blunt end of each bay or dead-end platform, or reception siding in a yard, there must be a red lamp facing the train as it approaches the buffer stops. This lamp is usually incorporated centrally into the crossbeam of the buffer stops, located centrally. The red lamp may just be a stand-ard red tail lamp fixed to a lamp bracket on the buffer stops.

Modellers who go for super-detailing their scenery may want to add to the realism by fitting dummy points rodding between the base of the nearest signal box and each box-worked point. At least one manufacturer, Wills, makes kits of these

for OO scale modellers (SS89). Stringing the signal arm pull wires on their posts and pulleys to connect the signal box to each semaphore signal is also an added detail option, which will probably need to be scratch-built.

COLOUR LIGHT AND MULTIPLE-ASPECT SIGNALS

THREE-ASPECT AND FOUR-ASPECT SYSTEMS

The simplest form of colour light signalling effectively replaces semaphore signals directly with lamps that

On 3 August 1959, a new train of 2-car EMUs leaves Bury Bolton Street en route to Manchester Victoria on the ex-L&YR DC side-contact conductor rail system. The train is passing the Down home signals that protect entry to four station platforms. These are searchlight signals in which a single lens and bulb have a set of coloured filters that change the colour of the emitted light in accordance with the signal aspect needed, in this case red on all tracks.

mimic the colours shown by the semaphore signals' oil lamps. Thus, a colour light home signal will have two aspects, red and green. A distant signal will have two aspects, red and yellow. A starter signal will also be two-aspect red and green, unless it is combined with the distant signal for a following block section, in which case it will have three aspects, the third being yellow. Some older colour light signals actually had just one lamp, covered internally as required by a red, yellow or green filter. This was on a rotatable disc that was motor-driven from the signal box to colour the light emitting from the lamp through the front lens.

The common type of fixed-lamp signalling is the more modern multiple-aspect signalling (MAS) that British Railways spread along its main and busy sec-ondary routes from the early 1960s onwards. While this system still uses the 'space interval' principle for train separation, in some ways it is simpler to understand than the semaphore system, and not difficult to model either.

MAS comes in two versions, the simpler being known as 'three-aspect' and the slightly more complex one as 'four-aspect'.

Along the open main line, the running line has signals spaced at intervals that recognize the maximum stopping distance of the trains running at the line speed limit on that route. In the three-aspect system, the three aspects are red, yellow and green. In all these signals, the red aspect is the bottom lamp, being closest to the line of vision of approaching train drivers; its position at the bottom is a help if the driver has to walk close to the signal to see what aspect, if any, is showing, either in thick fog or dazzling sunshine. On the running lines, the signals are usually automatic. As a train passes a signal, the signal turns to red, to protect that train from following trains. When the train passes the next signal, that signal then changes to red and the first signal changes to yellow, and as the train passes a third signal the first one changes to green. The aspects, as seen from an approaching train, mean much the same as the red, yellow and green do in a semaphore area: red means 'stop'; yellow means 'caution' – the next signal is red, so the driver must be prepared to stop at it; green means 'clear', indicating that the train can proceed at line speed, and that the next signal may be either green or yellow.

Ahead of a junction, up to two signals before the junction show a 'feather' of lights above the signal, seen by a train driver as a row of white lights pointing diagonally left for a left junction and diagonally right for a junction to the right. At a place where a signaller must intervene to control trains in a station, yard or series of junctions, the signals are the same visually, but locally they may not be fully automatic. Instead, they may be subject to control by a signaller, who is often at a remote location. MAS allows signals to be controlled from a long distance away, at a centralized signalling centre, and does away with many of the traditional signal boxes. Thus, on a model of a modern railway, a signal box need not always be modelled, even at a busy junction such as Derby or Trent. A modern signalling centre can

The three-aspect signal that the Class 87 electric locomotive is facing has added precautions because of the presence of 25kV overhead wires. There are two ladders to enable access to the lamps and wiring. The Class 303 EMU is held behind a pair of electric ground signals. This scene was recorded on 24 May 1983.

The modern Midland main line is four-aspect signalling territory along much of its length. At Harpenden on 25 April 1983, a Class 45 diesel pulls away under control of a double-yellow aspect, as an HST approaches on a Down fast service. Above the two yellow aspects is a left feather that is unlit because the 45 is heading straight along the Up main line.

look like an office block, and not be immediately identifiable as a railway building.

Older colour light signals can show a junction by using two signal heads side by side on a bracket on the same post.

Ground colour light signals show three aspects: one red light and one white light side by side indicates a stop instruction; two white lights at 45 degrees indicates a proceed aspect. A ground signal showing yellow and white lights horizontally has the same function as a yellow disc signal at 'caution'.

On high-speed railways where train headways need to be close, for example on a busy 125mph line or an outer suburban route where trains chase each other every three minutes or so, an extra 'section' is signalled by having four aspects on the automatic signals. As before, the bottom signal aspect is red, next up the signal head is yellow, then green, then a second yellow. Thus, the signal light sequence faced by a train can be green, double yellow, yellow, red. Four-aspect signalling enables the trains to run closer to each other, but the four stages allow for the normal stopping distances to be achieved. A development of this, which warns of a slower-speed diversion at a junction ahead, uses flashing green followed by flashing double yellow, then yellow and red aspects, or a final green if the diversion route is clear. The last signal sometimes clears as the train approaches on an 'approach control' system.

Three-aspect signalling.

Four-aspect signalling.

Indicates junction to the right.

Feather for junction (example).

MODELLING MAS

Early in his modelling hobby, one of our members decided that, from most viewing angles, the lights emitting from colour light signals on real railways are not visible to the human eye. Certainly, they are usually very faint, unless seen head-on from the train driver's viewpoint, which is where the lamp lenses are focused. For that reason, he decided not to bother with working model light signals, which greatly simplified the few signals he wanted to fit in on his small layout. He constructed each one from a plastic card head made up as a box and stuck round the top of a toffee-apple stick, with the lamp shades also modelled in 'five-thou' plastic card. He fitted a ladder formed from a metal item from the model trade. He painted the signal head and lamp shades black, and the posts silver (incorrectly, as the posts should have been white, with a black section near the ground). And no visitor to his model railway has ever commented that the signal aspects are not lit!

Commercially available model multiple-aspect signals do show a very bright light, particularly those using 'grain-of-wheat' bulbs. Better realism can be obtained with light-emitting diodes (LEDs), with resistances added in circuit to make them even more realistically dim to the eye.

Working model colour light signals are marketed, among others, by Hornby and Dapol (fairly basic), Berco, Eckon and Train Tech. Some are of overseas prototypes, but you need to be an expert to notice any significant difference from UK practice.

MAS requires some lineside equipment in place – usually a small clutch of silver- or grey-painted equipment cabinets situated at the lineside near some signals. They can easily be modelled as boxes in plastic card, but it is important to check photographs first for detail. These cabinets can be modernized by painting some model graffiti on them for added realism!

Bear in mind that the London Midland Region modernized its signalling across the board from its inherited semaphore signalling to full MAS during much of the time BR was in existence. If you are modelling the Midland Region in the 1950s and 1960s, semaphore signalling would dominate, apart from on the West Coast Main Line. The 1970s and 1980s saw widespread modernization in signalling, so it is essential to consider what area or station is being modelled, and then to study photographs taken in the area during the period being modelled.

TRAIN HEADCODES AND LAMPS

HEADLAMPS

On the Famous Trains layout, wherever possible, every train that would have displayed headlamps or discs in BR days carries them on the model, arranged in the correct code. Before the late 1950s, when DMUs began to display alphanumeric codes (see below), all trains showed a code of white headlamps or discs. The codes denoted the type of train (on all Regions except the Southern), to ensure that signallers and station staff knew how to handle each particular variant. (On the SR only, the codes showed the route on which the train was travelling.)

On the LM Region, all steam locomotives at front and rear carried four lamp irons, basically mild-steel brackets on which headlamps could be slotted, held in place by gravity. The lamp brackets were fitted, one at the top of the smokebox front, one on the front running board above the centre of the buffer beam, and one either side of it approximately above each buffer.

Locomotives that ran on the Southern Region at any time, such as BR Standard engines and a few LMR Class 5s and ER B1s that were loaned to the SR in 1953, also gained lamp brackets at either side of the smokebox door. Modern models of steam loco-

46203 awaits its next duty at Carlisle, an express passenger train for Scotland. The two white lamps it is carrying identify it as a Class A (later Class 1) train. This picture dates from the 1960s. Until the late 1950s, parts of the LM Region used black-painted headlamps, as can be seen in some other illustrations.

Brand-new English Electric Type 4 No D211 at Camden in May 1959, showing its four headcode discs, all with the lids closed. When a lid was opened and clipped up vertically, it uncovered a white-painted circular area. In the lower half of the disc was a white marker lamp to show the code at night. The two visible lamps on this locomotive are red tail lamps.

The first batches of Derby-built 'lightweight' DMUs had four marker lamps on the cab fronts as well as a destination indicator.

motives have these lamp brackets in place – they are very small indeed, even in OO scale!

BR policy was for headlamps to be painted all-over white. They emitted a white light when the oil wicks were lighted. Diesel locomotives delivered early in the BR Modernisation Plan had folding discs that showed a white disc when opened and uncovered a white electric lamp.

Because many trains ran from one railway or Region to another, the headcodes were generally standardized across the UK railways. For example, at the 1923 grouping, the Railway Clearing House issued a set of standard headcodes dividing trains into nine different classes, from A to K (omitting I); under BR, these became classes 1 to 9.

The earliest first-generation DMUs were delivered with either two, three or four marker lamps on the cab fronts. If only two lamps were fitted, they were normally both illuminated at night. From 1956, DMUs began to be delivered with two-digit

code boxes centrally on the cab front below the windscreens; illuminated at night, the box showed a letter denoting the class of train (for example, B for a stopping passenger train) and a number relating to the duty.

All LMR DMUs also had destination blinds showing where the train was going.

As signalling systems progressed with the Modernisation Plan, BR began using four-digit train describers in signal boxes. For a decade or so in the later 1960s to the 1980s, the train describer codes were displayed in lit boxes on later-built train fronts. For a list of the codes, *see* Appendix.

In 1976, the use of train-displayed headcodes was dropped by BR because the computerized signalling system was able to relay train describer information to signalling centres and 'boxes in real time. This was not long before the introduction of bright headlamps on trains, following which many code boxes on train fronts were either plated over or removed.

A: Express passenger, newspaper, breakdown train or snow plough going to clear line

B: Ordinary passenger, mixed train or breakdown train not going to clear line

C: Parcels, fish, empty coaching stock or freight/ballast train with not less than half vehicles braked

D: Express freight, livestock, ballast train with not less than one third of wagons braked

E: Express freight, livestock or ballast train with at least four auto braked vehicles next to engine

F: Express freight, livestock or ballast train not fitted with auto brake

G: Light engine or engines; engine with not more than two brake vans

H: Through freight or ballast train not under headcodes C, D, E or F

J: Mineral or empty wagon train

K: Freight, mineral or ballast train stopping at stations or in section

Royal train

Shunting engine

NB: BR later changed the code letters to numbers as follows: A = 1; B = 2; C = 3 and 4; D = 5; E = 6; F = 7; G = 0; H = 8; J = 9. Code K was combined with and included within Code J.

© 2017 Colin Boocock

Steam and early diesel headcodes.

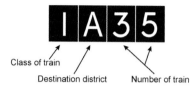

Class of train
Destination district
Number of train

Classes of trains:

1 - Express passenger, newspaper, breakdown train or snowplough going to clear the line
2 - Ordinary passenger train, mixed train or breakdown train not going to clear the line
3 - Parcels, fish, empty coaching stock

4 - Freight/ballast train with not less than half wagons braked

5 - Express freight, livestock, ballast train with not less than one third of wagons braked
6 - Express freight, livestock, ballast train with at least four braked wagons next to the engine
7 - Express freight or ballast train not fitted with auto brake

8 - Through freight or ballast train not under headcodes 4, 5, 6 or 7

9 - Freight, mineral, ballast or empty wagon train

0 - Light engine or engines; engine with not more than two brake vans

London Midland Region destination district codes:

A - London Euston; B - Euston or Rugby;
C - St Pancras, Marylebone, Manchester North; D - Chester, Nottingham;
F - Leicester; G - Birmingham; H - Manchester South, Stoke-on-Trent;
J - Manchester North; K - Crewe, Liverpool; L - Preston, Barrow, Carlisle;
L - Blackpool and Fylde, Derby

Inter-Regional destination codes:

E - Eastern; M - London Midland; N - North Eastern; O - Southern;
S - Scottish; V - Western

Special and excursion train codes:

X - Passenger and freight (inter-Regional)
T - Passenger (local to LM Region), trip freight
Z - Passenger and freight (local to LM Region)

Diesel and electric headcodes.

Some headcode boxes were changed to display two white circular discs, illuminated at night. These and others were mostly later plated over, once bright headlamps became standard in the late 1980s.

With many diesel and electric unit and locomotive classes having different types of headcode display built into them at different times, it is essential to refer to period photographs to make sure that individual models are correct.

One change that affected steam locomotives in the early 1960s was the spread of 25kV wiring overhead. As a precaution, on many locomotives the lamp bracket in front of the locomotive chimney was moved to the right side (looking at the locomotive front) of the smokebox door, so that the person placing a lamp there was not as close to immediate danger as before. At around the same time, several steam locomotives, deemed to be too tall, were barred from working south of Crewe under the wires. This was indicated by means of a broad yellow diagonal stripe across each cabside below the side windows.

Again, check photographs if you want to be correct at this level of detail.

TAIL LAMPS

In addition to headcode lamps, trains in the UK and elsewhere displayed red-emitting tail lamps at the

Arriving at Crewe from the Chester direction, this BRCW-built 3-car DMU shows its two-digit headcode display. B denotes an ordinary passenger train, and 2 is its duty number. This unit has just two marker lamps on the cab front.

Four-digit headcode displays became the norm for newly constructed trains from about 1961. This pair of Derby Class 108s approaching Bolton from Manchester displays just B0 at the front, suggesting the local area did not wish to use the full four-digit codes.

The correct code that this Class 40 should be showing as a light engine at Crewe station should be 0Z00. After 1976, these code display boxes would initially be covered in black vinyl, with a white disc in the centre. After locomotives began to be fitted with bright headlamps in the 1980s, the code boxes were blanked off or removed completely.

back of the train. The tail lamp served two distinct purposes. Its primary use was to enable signallers to check as trains went past that they were complete – in other words, that no vehicles had become uncoupled en route. The tail lamp was also intended to act as a warning for any train approaching from the rear. Tail lamps differed from headlamps in that the light they emitted was red.

A single tail lamp was generally employed in the UK in all situations except on freight trains with unfitted wagons, and where other local rules applied, as on the Tunstead–Northwich limestone trains. In addition to the red-emitting tail lamp, two lamps would be placed on brackets at the sides of the brake van, emitting a forward white light, so that the engine crew could look back and check that the train had not divided unintentionally. These side lamps also

emitted a red light to the rear as an additional safety measure. When such a train was looped, to enable a faster train to pass, it was recommended practice for the guard to turn one side lamp round to emit a rear-facing white light on the side adjacent to the faster running line. Thus the driver of an approaching train would know that the train seen to be in front was actually safely to one side and not in the line of potential collision,

Even DMUs and EMUs carried oil tail lamps right into the early 1970s, before BR became confident enough to rely on electric lamps built into the rear of the trains. In the later BR era, when freight trains were made up of air-braked wagons, brake vans were dispensed with. The modern tail lamp is battery-powered, and emits a flashing red light facing to the rear.

ROYAL TRAINS

A train carrying the monarch or senior members of the royal family had a special headcode in which four white headlamps sat on all four front lamp brackets. Also, a royal train displayed two tail lamps. In the four-digit era, the displayed code on the train front for a royal train was 1X01 (1X00 when running as empty stock).

SHUNTING LOCOMOTIVES

The only instance to our knowledge where a locomotive carried lamps at the front and the rear simultaneously (except when running light) was in shunting. This was also the only instance when red and white emitting lamps were used on both ends of a locomotive. Looking at the locomotive from the front, the red lamp was on the right and the white lamp on the left, with the same format at the rear.

MODELLING

Famous Trains uses the head and tail lamp models supplied by Springside, often bought through the very user-friendly Gaugemaster website. Springside sell dummy lamps in OO scale that are based on the four pre-1948 main railways, as well as BR.

DCC Concepts and other traders sell fully working head and tail lamps, if you have the patience to wire them up. The Heljan model of the LMS Beyer Garratt locomotive class already has a headlamp fitted at each end, lit in the direction of travel and fixed in the correct position to denote a heavy mineral train (such as the long coal trains on which they normally worked).

Fitting the Springside lamps is fiddly because they do not slot on to model locomotive lamp irons, which are in any case too small and fragile. Our practice is to glue them in position in front of the relevant lamp bracket on the model, with superglue if they are likely to be permanent, or something less strong if they are to be regularly removed or changed. (The surfaces on the lamps to be glued should be filed flat first, to remove moulding lines.)

CHAPTER NINE

ELECTRIFICATION AND INFRASTRUCTURE

THE DEVELOPMENT OF ELECTRIFICATION

Railway electrification has a long history in the British Isles and a significant part of the development has occurred within what became the London Midland Region of British Railways.

Although overhead electrification is probably the format most familiar outside the old Southern Region, the predecessors of the London Midland Region had significant lengths of conductor rail electrification, stemming from the Lancashire & Yorkshire Railway in the Manchester area, the Mersey Railway and Wirral electrifications in the Liverpool area, and the London & North Western Railway in the London area. This was mainly third rail at 650 volts, but the Manchester–Bury electrification was at 1,200 volts with side contact. In the London area, the arrangement was a four-rail system, nominally at 650 volts but with the third and fourth rails insulated from the running rails. The motivation behind this was integration with underground services in the capital on both the North London line and the suburban lines of the West Coast route. In the other systems, one running rail was used as the traction current return rail.

The 1,200-volt system was abandoned in 1991 when the route was converted to light rail as part of the Manchester Metrolink project, and tramway-style overhead line equipment was installed. The Liverpool system was developed and extended with the traditional third rail and traction return running rail system. In the London area, BR simplified the fourth rail system by converting it to third rail. However, shared running with London Underground was still required on certain sections of the routes and this was achieved by retaining the fourth rail in situ as a return conductor but electrically bonding it to the traction return running rail.

However, conductor rail electrification was not the main system chosen by British Railways for new electrification within the London Midland Region. Early main-line electrification in the United Kingdom used overhead catenary, usually at 1,500 volts. This was the system proposed in the Weir Report for the main lines in the 1930s and was initially seen to be the preferred system for electrification of the London Midland Region main lines. A 1,500-volt DC overhead system already existed on the Manchester, South Junction & Altringham lines, installed by the London Midland & Scottish Railway (1931), with a short stretch of the same system on the Woodhead route from Manchester to Sheffield, part of which was within the LM Region.

A unique system of overhead electrification had been used by the Midland Railway on the Lancaster, Morecambe and Heysham route using overhead conductors at 6.6kV AC. Following a review of French electrification practice, BR decided that the system with the best potential was industrial frequency AC overhead line. The Lancaster, Morecambe and Heysham route was duly converted to a 6.25kV AC overhead line system, mainly re-using the existing overhead line infrastructure. The standard French system used 25kV AC, but this required greater clearances and the lower voltage was more suitable for BR's trial purposes. Interestingly, ex-London & North Western Railway DC electric multiple units were fitted with pantograph collectors, as AC traction equipment with DC rectifiers was also installed. The results were positive and the decision was made to proceed with 25kV AC overhead electrification for the West Coast Main Line northwards from Euston, including the Birmingham and Northampton loops.

The scene was then set for what O.S. Nock described as 'Britain's New Railway', for this was also a complete rebuilding of the West Coast Main Line. It would include new track and foundations, power signalling and speed improvements, with modern telecommunications and control centres very much incorporating the newest technology of the time.

THE AC ELECTRIFICATION EQUIPMENT

For the modeller, the areas of interest are generally those to be physically modelled – in effect, what can be seen. The basis of the overhead line electrification system is the contact wire, which delivers the traction current to the train. The contact wire hanging from the supporting catenary wire is located by electrification structures, which hold it in place over

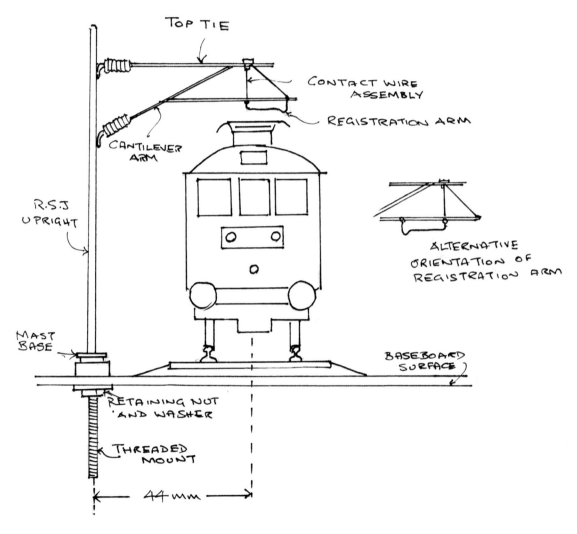

The basic structure for electrification, the single-track cantilever. This particular sketch is of the Mark 3 format, but the basic principle applies. Mark 3 equipment appears on the second phase of the West Coast electrification to Glasgow in the 1970s. This structure is modelled by Peco in their 4mm scale range.

the track. Traction current is fed through feeder cables and switchgear through that contact wire. The power is then used on the train and fed back through a running rail to the source. The return path in the original scheme was through another wire called the return conductor and then back to the substation or feeding location. The contact wire is divided into discrete sections called tension lengths, which are no more than 1,500 metres apart. At the end of each length, the wire is taken to one side out of running, while the next tension length is brought in from a structure to the rear. The non-live arms of the system are bonded to the relevant running rail.

Further infrastructure items included structure-mounted transformers called booster transformers, and manual switches to enable staff to isolate the system section by section. The modeller must take a view as to how much of the equipment will be represented as, depending on the scale, some of the infrastructure items will be very small in dimension and almost invisible in the smaller scales.

The original London Midland Region overhead electrification equipment was designated Mark I and is distinctive in appearance. Structures were of cantilever type, either single- or double-track, and, for areas where the contact systems of several lines were to be supported, the structure was like

A portal typical of the first stage of the West Coast LM Region electrification. Known as a 'welded rod' structure, this was introduced by British Insulated Callender cables and was the standard format for multi-track installations. The contact system itself is of compound construction, with the third wire between contact and catenary wires. In this case, the catenary is supported over the beam but there are also cases of the catenary being supported under the beam. GLEN WILES

A head-span overhead line structure. This style of multi-track support for the contact system was developed and installed on the West Coast Main Line north of Weaver junction as part of the process of bringing the cost of electrification down. The beam of the portal structure has been replaced with the wire supports and the third wire of a compound system is no longer installed. GLEN WILES

an overbridge and was known as a 'portal'. A basic contact wire system consisted of a catenary wire supporting the contact wire by connections known as 'droppers', all held in place by steelwork and copper structural items, insulated in this earlier system by ceramic insulators.

As the Region's electrification was extended in the 1970s on the West Coast Main Line, there had been much work on reducing costs and, instead of the solid cross-track portals, structures known as head spans were introduced. These consisted of steel channel verticals with cross-track spans of wire supporting the contact system. Although less

costly, this arrangement had the disadvantage of dislocating the contact system across all lines if any head-span wire was damaged.

MODELLING ELECTRIFICATION EQUIPMENT

OVERHEAD LINE EQUIPMENT

There has been a considerable growth in the availability of models of electric traction but some of the modelling aids towards the contact system have been of dubious appearance. Early commercial OO scale versions were either oversimplified, like the single wire of the Trix and later Hornby systems, or of massive proportion, as with some pressed catenary/contact wire pieces. Model equipment has been available from mainland Europe from companies such as Sommerfeldt, but this has generally been more of continental European appearance.

Peco have introduced electrification equipment of UK type with catenary, dropper and contact wire parts. This is of the Mark 3 variety, which exists at the northern end of the West Coast Main Line and on Bedford–St Pancras. This model group currently includes only single-track cantilevers, but it is of a reasonable appearance and is robust. Dapol have also produced components – single-track cantilevers only at this stage. A further source of overhead line equipment has been that from the N Brass company, which is basically manufactured for N gauge but has also been scaled up to OO scale.

The Peco system is readily available and illustrations of how to install it have been published by both the company but also in the model railway press. The system comprises two distinct component sets – masts and catenary contact wires – all of which are factory assembled. The single masts are supplied complete with baseplate, cantilever arms, registration arm and dummy insulator pots. The catenary contact wires – wire frets representing the main catenary wire and the droppers – are supplied in five different lengths to enable the catenary to be installed around curves of different radii. A starter pack is available which includes twelve masts, installation jigs and a fully illustrated installation guide (Peco LC-150).

The Peco product closely resembles the Mark 3 cantilever design. This design will reasonably suit any part of the LM Region where single-track cantilevers are used. Peco are considering the introduction of portal structures, but this has not yet been confirmed. On a model railway, where the overhead line-equipped track goes off scene to a fiddle yard, the contact wire can be sloped upwards to enable a train's pantograph to raise to its full height, with the wire then terminated to avoid the presence of wires in an area where handling of stock is likely to take place.

THIRD RAIL DC EQUIPMENT

As in overhead electrification, there are many details that can be included when modelling a third rail system. Where there may be access for railway personnel to the track, a form of guard boarding is used either side of a conductor rail. On the Manchester–Bury 1,200V DC system, the whole route was boarded because of the higher voltage. There are also runs of parallel cables alongside the permanent way, acting as conductor rail feeders and also as continuity connections between lengths of conductor rail.

On DC railways there are frequent feeder stations supplying power to the conductor rail, both substations and also switching stations, known as track paralleling huts. The buildings may be of modern format or brick-built, sometimes of quite classic designs. Many are of a utilitarian brick-built design.

For the third rail options, Peco now produce insulators (conductor rail chairs), which could also be extended to cover the less common four rail system. These detailed mouldings are available as a pack of 100 and slide-fit on to Peco code 60 rail. A separate baseplate is included to allow for different rail heights. A conductor rail system is not, of course, continuous, and gaps are required for switch and crossings. The rail will also change sides, particularly in station platforms, where the rail will be on the opposite side of the running rails to the platform face. At the end of a conductor rail length there is a ramp to be formed, which may be done by slightly bending the rail down about a sleeper spacing length. The Peco code 60 rail is not an exact match for scale conductor rail but this is not noticeable in OO scale.

Fine scale options are available. The Scalefour Society commissioned Exactoscale to produce scale conductor rail supports of etched format and injection-moulded plastic, to accompany its correct scale section 150lb/yard conductor rail. These components are available only to Scalefour Society members, but can be purchased at Scalefour Society exhibitions.

C & L Finescale have produced conductor rail system parts, and this range includes items such as guard boarding, as well as jigs for installation. As ever, the fine scale systems will be more challenging to model, and it is likely that the Peco system will come to be seen as the optimum for the average UK modeller.

DEPOTS

LM Region traction maintenance depots had provision for working platforms and pits to allow repairs and maintenance to be undertaken. Servicing sheds were provided on the Midland line, for example at Wellingborough, which were really fuelling sheds, and these were of a fairly standard type. On the West Coast route, diesel depots were rather more of a make-do conversion, as the main aim was to electrify the route at an early date, and the depot designs were developed to suit that purpose.

The electric traction depots were very much of a common architecture and often combined the local electrical control room and electrification infrastructure maintenance base. Several depots were built along the West Coast route, but later it was realized that there had been an over-provision and some facilities were turned over to on-track plant maintenance. The depots were of open and modern appearance; the one at Willesden is a typical example. Similar depot buildings have been made available by Hornby and Bachmann in their resin buildings series and Corgi have produced a very typical crane in BR maroon.

For modellers of the steam era, there are many engine shed models and kits to choose from, some from the mainstream manufacturers and others from kit firms such as Metcalfe.

THE FAMOUS TRAINS
MODEL RAILWAY

The Famous Trains Model Railway is the only model railway in the UK that is open to the public in a free park. Visitors to Derby's Markeaton Park, off the north-west side of the city's ring road, can come into the Famous Trains building and see OO and other scale trains running every Saturday, Sunday and Monday between 11am and 4pm. This novel idea was the brainchild of two retired railway engineers, Colin Boocock and Peter Stanton, who wanted to give something back to society after enjoying fulfilling careers in engineering on the real railway.

The Famous Trains exhibition building is dominated by a large OO scale model railway based on Chinley station in Derbyshire as it was in the 1950s and 1960s. At that time, Chinley station had four main-line tracks running through it. The main line was that from London St Pancras to Manchester Central via Derby, and the other two tracks were formed by the Hope Valley line from Sheffield to Manchester. The station was busy with interconnecting passenger trains and heavy freights, and this model railway is buzzing with train movements,

The Famous Trains model railway hall in Derby, with the large Chinley OO scale railway on the left, and several smaller layouts on the right. The building was refurbished in 2013, opened to the public in April 2014, and received over 30,000 visitors in the following four years. It attracts not only railway enthusiasts but also many families who are passing by on their way in or out of Markeaton Park.

Realism in miniature: the Darley Mills factory complex has its own shunting engine, an ancient Peckett 0-4-0ST (a repainted Hornby), named in memory of a popular late FT member. The model factory buildings are mainly made up from Metcalfe card building kits.

with trains working along the four main lines and also from a loop platform, a short bay, and of course in and out of the goods yard.

Starting late in 2006, Colin and Peter set up a group of like-minded enthusiasts to take the project forward. They quickly gained registered charity status because they planned to educate the public with displays explaining the historical importance of Derby as a railway centre, and the role of the railways in the development of the Derbyshire limestone industry. The charity also planned to train volunteers in useful skills that would enhance their employability.

By mid-2013, the trustees had successfully negotiated with Derby City Council a 15-year lease of an ideal building that had a clear floor space of 22 metres by 8 metres. With grants from bodies such as Biffa Award and the Big Lottery Fund, they appointed a local contractor to upgrade the building. Three years earlier, the charity had been very fortunate indeed to be gifted a large model railway by the late Derek Chandley, who planned to 'upgrade' to O gauge at his home. This is how the model of Chinley station came into Famous Trains' possession – and the reason why there is a model public house on the layout named after Derek.

After taking over the building in November 2013 the members, by then nearly seventy in number, rewired the Chinley layout, extended it to achieve a minimum curve radius of 5 feet, and set about developing the scenic area around the station. Back in 2011 and 2012, members had built two small exhibition layouts to help promote the charity. These were designed subsequently to connect with each other and with Chinley, so that a branch line from the imaginary village of Darley Green would feed the Chinley station loop platform. It was not prototypical, but it was potentially an extra source of interest. An extension of the model railway in the other direction includes a canal basin with a working model of a rope-worked incline rising above it, representing the iconic Cromford & High Peak Railway. A quarry is also planned for this area.

The centre was first opened to the public on a regular weekend basis in April 2014. In the four years since then, it has welcomed about 30,000 visitors through the doors. Visitors to Famous Trains see about five different model railways of several gauges. The smallest is the miniature railway circuit in the fairground between Darley Green and Chinley, which is a Z gauge train with OO scale carriage bodies and riders. Visitors can set this running with a push-button. Plans are also afoot to set up a gauge 3 shuttle line along one wall of the building.

Famous Trains members run a mixture of trains on the Chinley layout. Most are typical London Midland Region trains of the area, including two sets of sixteen ICI bogie hopper wagons, one loaded, the other empty, which took limestone from the big quarry at Tunstead to the chemical works at Northwich in Cheshire. These unique model wagons were scratch-built by trustee Peter Swift. Coal trains off the Hope Valley line bring 8F, 9F and Garratt locomotives to Chinley with their loads of forty mineral wagons.

The Famous Trains team also runs trains that were foreign to the Chinley area, to keep to the theme of 'famous trains'. One popular star is the Silver Jubilee, which looks surprisingly modern for a 1935 streamlined train and attracts admiration from children as well as older adults. The Bourne-mouth Belle is the longest passenger train operated, with its twelve Pullman cars, and the Flying Scotsman set is probably the most famous train – apart, perhaps, from Thomas the Tank Engine (which appears only occasionally). Another theme that is partially developed is to run 'modern trains' from the twenty-first century, even though the model of Chinley station represents it before BR heavily rationalized the prototype in the 1980s to just one island platform.

Wartime trains are run during November each year, to coincide with Remembrance weekends.

Very young visitors usually make a bee-line for the wooden and plastic toy railway tracks, which they can play with safely. Model railway enthusiasts find bargains on the second-hand table, and of course everyone has to pass through the Famous Trains shop during their visit!

The Famous Trains charity has a comprehensive web site at www.famoustrains.org.uk as well as an active page at Facebook/Famous Trains.

LNWR lower quadrant signals and water cranes at the Crewe end of Chester General station on 10 June 1967.

LIST OF SUPPLIERS

LOCOMOTIVES AND ROLLING STOCK

Hornby Hobbies
Locomotives and rolling stock, buildings and line-side equipment.

Margate, Kent (widely available in all model shops and on line)
www.hornby.com/uk-en

Bachmann UK
Locomotives and rolling stock, buildings and line-side equipment.

Barwell, Leicestershire (widely available in all model shops and online) www.bachmann.co.uk

Dapol
Locomotives and rolling stock. Lineside kits.

Chirk, nr Wrexham (widely available in model shops and online)
www.dapol.co.uk

Heljan
Locomotives.

Denmark (available in many model shops and online from Hattons or Rails of Sheffield for example)

DJModels
Locomotives.

Available in many model shops and online
www.djmodels.co.uk

South East Finecast
White-metal locomotives.
www.sefinecast.co.uk

Kernow
1-Co Co 1 model
www.kernowmodelrailcentre.com

BUILDINGS AND SCENERY

Metcalfe models
Card kits www.metcalfemodels.com

Yorkshire (available in most model shops and online)

Superquick – card kits. www.superquick.co.uk
Bristol – available in most model shops and online.

Model Railway Scenery
Downloadable kits and laser-cut items.

Available online
www.modelrailwayscenery.com

Scalescenes
Downloadable models.

Available online
www.scalescenes.com

Ratio
Plastic kits.

Available in most model shops and online
www.peco-uk.com

Wills
Plastic kits and materials.

Available in most model shops and online
www.peco-uk.com

Petite Properties
Model buildings.

Available online
www.petiteproperties.com

L Cut
Laser-cut models.

Available online
www.lcut.co.uk

Peco
General railway modelling items.

Available in most model shops and online
www.peco-uk.com

Woodland Scenics
Wide range of scenic materials.

Available in many model shops and online
www.woodlandscenics.com

Javis
Wide range of scenic materials.

Available in many model shops and online
www.javis.co.uk

LINESIDE AND ACCESSORIES

Langley
White-metal kits.

Available in many model shops and online
www.langley-models.co.uk

Craftline
Balsa models for canals.

Available in many model shops and online
www.scalelink.co.uk

Mike's Models
White-metal lineside accessories.

Available in some model shops and online
www.mikes-models.co.uk

Duncan Models
White-metal lineside accessories.

Available in some model shops and online
www.duncanmodels.co.uk

C and L Finescale
Track making parts. Now including Exactoscale items.

Available online and at model shows
www.finescale.org.uk

ELECTRIFICATION AND SIGNALS

Sommerfeldt
Based on the continent and continental in style, available in specialist retailers or online

www.eurorailhobbies.com/sommerfeldt.asp

N Brass
All suitable items for overhead and third rail electrification in N gauge.

Available online
www.nbrasslocos.co.uk

Model Signal Engineering
Midland Railway signals, etc.
www.wizardmodels.ltd

Train Tech
Colour light signals.
www.train-tech.com

Traintronics
Colour light signals.
www.traintronics.co.uk

Eckon
Colour light signals.

Based on the continent but available online
www.onlinemodelsltd.co.uk

USEFUL SOURCES OF INFORMATION ABOUT THE REGION

London and North Western Railway Society
(www.lnwrs.org)

Lancashire and Yorkshire Railway Society
(www.lyrs.org.uk)

Cumbrian Railways Association
(www.cumbrianrailways.org.uk)

North Staffordshire Railway Study Group
(www.nsrsg.org.uk)

Midland Railway Society
(www.midlandrailway.org.uk)

LMS Society
(www.lmssociety.org.uk)

HMRS (Historical Model Railway Society)
(www.hmrs.org.uk)

INDEX

RELATED TITLES FROM CROWOOD

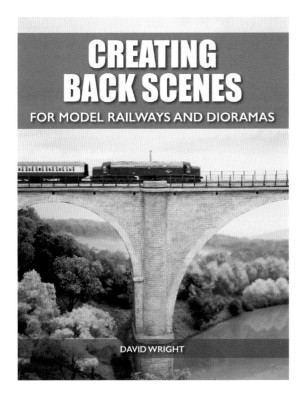

CREATING BACK SCENES FOR MODEL RAILWAYS AND DIORAMAS

DAVID WRIGHT

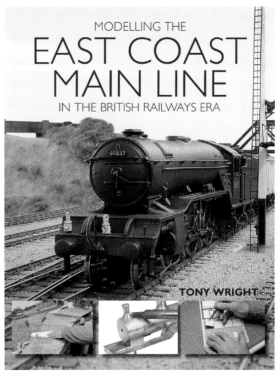

MODELLING THE EAST COAST MAIN LINE IN THE BRITISH RAILWAYS ERA

TONY WRIGHT

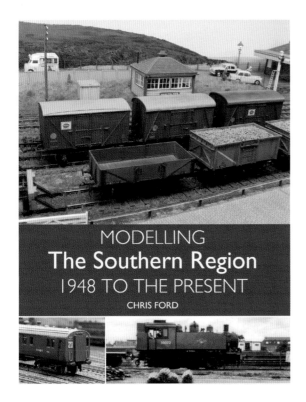

MODELLING The Southern Region 1948 TO THE PRESENT

CHRIS FORD

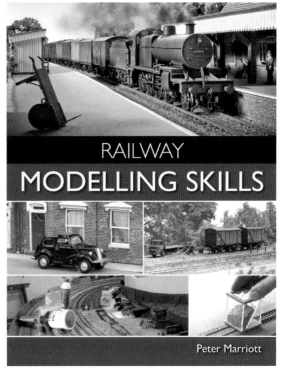

RAILWAY MODELLING SKILLS

Peter Marriott